NATIONAL ACCLAIM FOR *EMPTY ARMS* AND THE *EMPTY ARMS JOURNAL*

"Pam captures the heart of what women experience when losing a baby. Her willingness to share her story is an inspiration! The practical advice and wisdom found in *Empty Arms* is second to none."

Dr. Gary Smalley
Family counselor, best-selling author
As seen on Oprah Winfrey, Larry King Live, Extra, and the NBC Today Show

"Pam Vredevelt's *Empty Arms Journal* is an indispensable tool for wading through the heart wrenching pain of a miscarriage to find hope. I clung to Pam's first edition of Empty Arms like a life raft after my miscarriage. It was passed down to me by my aunt, who had also been given the book during her time of loss, and I've since passed it to a friend who has done the same. Our copy is well loved and wellworn, having been stained with countless tears, pages dogeared and many passages underlined highlighted or circled. The *Empty Arms Journal* now expands upon the richness of Pam's guidance, allowing the reader to fully engage in the healing process, also aiding the reinforcement of key concepts, encouragement and scripture. Pam's words and exercises provide optimal support, feeling like you're being wrapped in love while at your loneliest."

Katie Harman Ebner
Miss America 2002 and Acclaimed Classical Vocalist / Lyric Soprano

"Pam is my friend and I trust her. She is also brilliant, professional, intuitive and compassionate. Her work is not theoretical. She knows personally the heartbreak about that which she speaks and writes. As a result, what she offers in the *Empty Arms Journal* is deeply helpful. The challenge: you will not come to healing without your participation. You must do the hard work."

Wm Paul Young
Author of *The Shack, Cross Roads, Eve*

"Where do you turn when you suffer the deep and very personal loss of a baby? *Empty Arms*, offers tender words of hope and wisdom for those in grief. Pam Vredevelt's keen insight into the physical, emotional, and spiritual impact of losing a baby brings peace and comfort to broken hearts. After four miscarriages, I seriously wondered if I'd ever NOT be sad. I wish I had known about *Empty Arms*. I highly recommend this book!"

Lisa Jacobson
Founder of *Club 31 Women* blog, award winning author

"A healing path through grief, the *Empty Arms Journal,* is a road map to assist in rewiring the brain. Grief affects every nerve system in the body. Recovery from deep loss is like healing from a physical injury, though deeper and more difficult to grasp. Coordinated exercise of both the emotional memory and expressive brain circuits has been proven to help heal deep grief. Pam Vredevelt, an understanding therapist who has personally walked this course more than once, crafted this workbook. With expertise, she leads the reader through the steps of embracing loss and reshaping emotional pain. Using multiple methods of sensory expression and solid scriptural reflections,this workbook provides hours of comforting regrowth for the spirit and mind. Healing is clearly aided by engaging expressive output from the brain. I have carefully reviewed the content of this guidebook and strongly recommend it as a recovery tool within a Christian framework. This book will assist any believer struggling with the deep wounds of loss of an infant or child."

Warner B. Swarner, M.D.
Clinical Psychiatrist, Portland, Oregon

"Healing from a miscarriage or stillbirth is a complicated process, and having walked that road with several close friends, I know how essential Pam's counsel is. Both from personal and professional experience, she has been beautifully equipped to help the process of healing—physically, spiritually, and emotionally. Girded with biblical truth, this book will resonate with and help many, many readers."

Shaunti Feldhahn
Social researcher and best-selling author of *For Women Only*

"Pam's ability to relate with women suffering the trauma of pregnancy loss, and to guide them through the healing process is amazing! The best people to help us heal are always those who fully understand and empathize with our hurt."

Michael Smalley
CEO of Smalley Institute.

Professional counselor Pam Vredevelt knows the personal heartache of losing a child. *Empty Arms Journal* is strategic for moving forward in your healing process.

W. Terry Whalin
Author of more than 60 books including
Billy Graham, a Biography of America's Greatest Evangelist.

EMPTY
ARMS
Journal

21 Days of Good Grief Exercises for Healing After
Miscarriage, Stillbirth, and the Loss of a Baby

PAM VREDEVELT

EMPTY ARMS JOURNAL
21 Days of Good Grief Exercises for Healing After
Miscarriage, Stillbirth, and the Loss of a Baby

LIGHT SOURCE BOOKS
1326 NW Civic Dr
Gresham, OR 97030

The *Empty Arms Journal* provides information of a general nature and is not to be used as an alternative method for conditions requiring the services of a personal physician or other health-care professional.

Information contained in this book or in any other publication, article, or Web site should not be considered a substitute for consultation with a board-certified doctor to address individual medical needs. Individual facts and circumstances will determine the treatment that is most appropriate. The *Empty Arms Journal* publisher and its author, Pam Vredevelt, disclaim any liability, loss, or damage that may result in the implementation of the contents of this book.

Scripture quotations marked NLT are taken from the Holy Bible, New Living Translation. © 1996, 2004. Used by permission of Tyndale House Publishers, Inc., Wheaton, Illinois 60189. All rights reserved.

Scripture quotations marked MSG are from The Message by Eugene Peterson. © 1993, 1994, 1995, 1996, 2000, 2001, 2002. Used by permission of NavPress Publishing Group. All rights reserved.

Scripture quotations marked NASB are from the New American Standard Bible. © The Lockman Foundation, 1960, 1962, 1963, 1968, 1971, 1972, 1973, 1975, 1977, 1995. Used by permission.

Scripture quotations marked NKJV are from the New King James version. © 1982 by Thomas Nelson, Inc. Used by permission. All rights reserved.

Scripture quotations taken from the Amplified Bible (AMP), Copyright © 2015 by the Lockman Foundation. Used by permission. www.Lockman.org

Library of Congress Cataloging-in-Publication Data:
Empty Arms Journal: 21 Days of Good Grief Exercises for Healing After Miscarriage, Stillbirth, and the Loss of a Baby. By Pam Vredevelt.

Includes bibliographical references and index.

Cover and Interior Design | Yvonne Parks | www.PearCreative.ca

ISBN 978-0-9976876-0-6

This book is dedicated to all the moms and dads who have landed, more abruptly than they could ever imagine, in the Valley of Shadows.

Pleasure comes and goes, but joy has eternity in it.
HEATHER KING

I deeply appreciate the feedback I receive from my readers. It helps others to make an informed decision before buying my book. If you find value in the pages ahead, please consider leaving a brief review on amazon.com at:
http://a.co/9AWv2Cf

CONTENTS

FREE VIDEOS AND MP3 DOWNLOADS FOR HEALING AFTER PREGNANCY LOSS AVAILABLE AT PAMVREDEVELT.COM

ACKNOWLEDGEMENTS

A book of this sort does not happen without the love, support, and influence of many significant people. First, I want to thank my husband, John, for his consistent encouragement and cheerleading over 40 years of marriage to keep sharing my message.

I also want to express my gratitude to the people who have generously made extraordinary contributions of their time, energy, and resources.

Liz Haney and Traci Mullins shared their expert editing skills to help create a book that is changing people's lives. They edit for the most talented writers in the industry and I'm humbled they made time to work with me on this project. Yvonne Parks sacrificed long hours to create an amazing, artistic presentation of the text that breathes peace and comfort into weary souls. Her gifting is simply phenomenal.

Gail Gunstone provided detailed proofing and valuable feedback for refinements that make the journal very user friendly. This eagle-eye encourager fanned my flames right down to the midnight hour of the publication deadline. Side by side we peered at the screen together into the wee hours of the morning making final touches. Once the manuscript was in, her husband, Don, whisked the four of us away to rest and recharge in the beauty of the San Juan Islands. He also sponsored books to key influencers and groups that assist women who have lost a baby. Their lives inspire and challenge me to be a more generous giver.

Joy Marsh worked diligently to corral unruly commas, misspelled words, and redundant statements. She found bloopers my eyes never saw during several careful readings of the manuscript. Her tedious proofing was invaluable! Chuck Walker, and Sharon Correll also discovered ways to enhance clarity and improve content delivery with their insightful comments and questions during the book's development.

Alyssa Avant and Beth and Oliver Waller helped launch our online community at pamvredevelt.com and the Pam Vredevelt Author Facebook forum. Their ongoing, timely feedback and creative strategies are helping to reach more moms and dads who have suffered the devastating loss of a baby.

I want to thank those who have mentored me through my own grief journey – those who have taught me face to face and from afar the best practices to promote healing: My father, Charles S. Walker, Jerry Cook, C.S. Lewis, Lewis Smedes, Pamela Reeve, H. Norman Wright, Wm. Paul Young, Jerry Sittser, Elisabeth Kübler-Ross, Harold Kushner, Diane Landberg, David Kessler, Phillip Yancey, Randy Alcorn, Brene Brown, and my brain science research comrades who continually press forward in the lab to unveil effective ways to embrace our pain and heal our heart.

WELCOME TO A HEALING PATH THROUGH GRIEF

When your dreams crash into reality, a season of mourning begins.

Losing a baby touches every part of your life. Your view of yourself. Your relationships. Your hopes and fears about the future. Your wallet. Your dreams. Your beliefs about life and death—and God.

Crossing the threshold into the Valley of Shadows thrusts you into a stark awareness of the uncertain nature of this world. You have no clue what is around the next bend.

At some point, each of us must make this long, arduous trek through the dark. It's common for moms to enter this dreadful valley pitifully unprepared. I know I did. Following the sudden death of our baby, and years later, our sixteen-year-old son, I found myself thinking, *No one told me the path would be this steep, this rocky, this long, this black.*

Awakened to the priceless value of life and seared by the persistent ache of empty arms, we are dazed by sadness. There are moments when we wonder if we'll survive. Debilitating loneliness descends. We feel alone because we've been left behind. Inconsolable longings fill the empty spaces in our soul. We feel alone because we don't believe that others truly understand our pain.

Grief is hard emotional work. After dragging ourselves through basic responsibilities and routines, we have little energy left over to socialize. So we withdraw. When our heart is buried in sharp rubble we don't feel like interacting or putting on a pleasant face. It feels so fake. Knowing we'll be poor company, we sometimes retreat. Other times, we simply don't have enough energy to care about anything.

Grief takes a toll. It's like the dynamic force of an extreme roller coaster ride that slams us every which way and sucks the air clean out of us. Trauma fog clouds our perception. We're left dizzy, reeling with confusion, making it difficult to think straight or focus. Pain persists. Sadness won't budge. Time and again we wonder, *Where's the exit sign out of this horrible place?*

Accepting death and suffering is part of our spiritual journey. Significant loss tests our faith. Grief tends to hinder our ability to sense God's presence. We wonder where He is, and why He didn't show up to write a different ending to our story.

In what feels like a God-forsaken place, we are faced with critical choices of the will: Will we give death the final say and hold onto despair? Or will we believe that there is more going on than meets the eye, and that somehow God will bring life out of death, for our highest good and His highest glory? Will we invite God's companionship or shut Him out of our journey? Will we trust God to orchestrate a way through the darkness, or will we light our own way?

Loss is not a simple affair. It is fraught with multiple layers of meaning. Will we take the time we need to face and embrace our pain and let it go? Even as we rightfully grieve, will we trust that God is planting seeds of new life in the cracks of our broken heart? Will we believe His promise to transform our loss? To bring life out of death and make all things new?

> *He that lacks time to mourn, lacks time to mend.*
> MAYA ANGELOU

During the years of my darkest grief, I spent long hours alone with God, reading, reflecting, and filling journals. Together, we did the hard work of healing and letting go. Powerful yearnings drew my heart toward heaven. It seemed like I lived with one foot in this world and one foot in the next, poised between faith and doubt, relief and regret, hope and great sadness. In the solitude of communion with God, the space between heaven and earth narrowed. Glimmers of holy light pierced through, alerting me to insights, meaning, and whispers of purpose. My hope now is that my experience can help you on your own path through the valley and give you encouragement along the way. Each of us must make the arduous journey ourselves, but sometimes it's helpful to have a hand to hold.

Writing to Heal

Our minds are designed to try to understand the things that happen to us. When we suffer the loss of a baby either before or after birth, we work overtime to make sense of the experience and find meaning. Writing allows us to pause and intentionally focus on the significant things that matter most to us. We step back, pay attention, and sort through our experiences. By translating our loss into language and putting a pen to paper, we engage in good grief. Our loss seems more manageable.

Turns out that there is a lot of scientific evidence to support the therapeutic value of journaling after a traumatic loss. Brain SPECT Imaging shows us that the act of writing accesses the left brain, which is analytical and rational. While the left brain is occupied, the right brain is free to perceive, create, and feel. Writing clears the mind of mental blocks and helps us to tap into more brainpower to creatively think matters through and sort things out.

People who write about their traumatic experiences report improved memory, less depression, more happiness, fewer trips to the doctor, and overall improved health. Those who journal feel happier and less negative than before they write. Depressive symptoms, ruminations, and general anxiety tend to drop in the weeks and months after writing occurs.[1] Multiple studies show that writing helps us come to terms with trauma and reduces its negative impact on our physical health.[2] It strengthens immune cells and can decrease symptoms of asthma and rheumatoid arthritis.[3] People who write about their experiences after being diagnosed with Post-Traumatic Stress Disorder (PTSD) report fewer flashbacks, nightmares, and intrusive painful memories. This enables them to slowly reconnect to activities and places that they'd otherwise avoid.[4]

THE POSITIVE IMPACT OF FOCUSED WRITING

The effect of two types of journaling were compared during a one-month study.

- One group wrote about their deep feelings related to a personal trauma.
- A second group recorded their deep feelings and thoughts about their trauma.
- A third group focused their writing on factually reporting events.
- Results: Journaling about a personal trauma facilitated positive growth. However, the focus of journaling was important. Writing that expressed emotions and thoughts while trying to make sense of the trauma, with a focus on looking for the positive gifts inherent in suffering, showed significantly greater benefits than journaling focused strictly on the expression of painful emotion. Writers who focused on painful emotion alone reported more symptoms of illness during the study.

Even writing for only twenty minutes a day can rewire the brain and facilitate healing.[6] The purpose of the *Empty Arms Journal* is to offer a guided step-by-step process that will empower you to successfully work through your grief. As you write, you will discover new insights, inspirations, and capacities that will keep you moving forward *through* the shadows, without getting stuck.

I've seen the sticking power of unresolved grief. I'll never forget Sarah, who came to see me because her medical doctor insisted. She was struggling with chronic depression. Joy and fulfillment had been chased away long ago by a persistent black mood. "It feels like I'm always sad and worried, and I don't know what to do about it," she lamented.

I learned that Sarah had given birth to a stillborn baby many years before. After leaving the hospital she had not discussed it again. "It doesn't do any good to dredge up the past. It makes things worse, not better," she said, almost robotically. When I asked if she would tell me about her baby, it was like the event had happened just yesterday. The dam broke and years of bottled-up grief poured out. She had carried that heavy weight all alone for many years.

Things changed that day. Sarah put words to her story and took an important step on the road of healing.

How to Use This Journal

Sarah is one of the many beautiful women who inspired this healing journal. They wondered: *Where can I find relief from the overwhelming sadness? What does healthy grief look like? Where do I start? How long will it take?* They wanted signs, markers, and footprints to follow. If you've found yourself asking such questions, this guide is for you.

The *Empty Arms Journal* is divided into twenty-one days. Each day you will use a five-step process for successfully engaging and letting go of grief. You will:

- Listen to Your Heart
- Linger in the Light
- Look for the Good
- Lift Up Thanks
- Lighten Your Load

You are more resilient than you may think. Incorporating these practices into your life can prompt a keen awareness of God's presence with you and position you to receive fresh, daily doses of comfort, insight, and renewal. As you pause to pay attention to inner longings, open your heart to receive God's healing love, and use the time-tested practices offered, you'll develop vital resources that fortify your resolve, nurture resilience, help you adapt to a new normal, and slowly but surely reclaim your joy.

THE ADVANTAGES OF JOURNALING

Those who practice journaling:

- are re-employed sooner after losing their jobs

- miss fewer days of work

- have higher grade point averages

- show better overall sporting performances

- have better working memories. [7]

I invite you to participate in whatever way you are comfortable and at your own pace. Be gentle with yourself. This is not a time to push hard. You can move through the material in twenty-one days or stretch it out over several months. Use one tool a day, a few, or all five. The right choice is whatever works best for you. If something is too painful, remind yourself that you are safe and you can stop writing any time you want. Return when you have the energy to do so.

Along with space to answer specific questions related to your loss, there are plenty of blank pages for you to creatively release your grief. Write, draw, color, attach meaningful photos, mementos, or clip art. Let this be your personal way of honoring and capturing the essence of the baby you lost, and preserving the memories around his or her brief life with you. The choices are all yours.

It's time to begin your healing journey.

I will walk alongside you.

You are not alone.

BONUS VIDEO

Your Story Matters!
https://youtu.be/hLIGKh8yVDc

Good Grief

- The common, intensely painful, mental and physical response to loss.
- Intense and dominant thoughts, feelings, and behaviors occur erratically and vary over time
- Blend of yearning and deep sadness
- Shorter attention span than usual
- Accompanying thoughts and memories of the death, and the deceased person
- A tendency to be more interested in your inner world than activities of ordinary life
- Most people move along this painful and challenging road of grief to eventually accept their loss and see a future that has joy and satisfaction. When this transformation does not occur within the first couple of years, reach out for help to prevent Complicated Grief or Prolonged Grief Disorder.

Complicated Grief

Prolonged Grief Disorder (PGD) exists when 5 or more symptoms are present after six months have elapsed since the loss. The distress causes impairment in functioning socially, on the job, or other areas of responsibility such as home life:

- Confusion about one's role in life or a diminished sense of self
- Difficulty accepting the loss
- Avoidance of reminders of the reality of the loss
- Lowered trust in others since the loss
- Bitterness or anger related to the loss
- Difficulty moving on with life (ie. making new friends, pursuing interests)
- Feeling that life is unfulfilling, empty, or meaningless since the loss
- Feeling stunned, dazed or shocked by the loss
- The distress has been assessed is not a function of major depression, generalized anxiety, or Post-Traumatic Stress Disorder. [8]

DAY ONE
Reeling from the Shocking News

TODAY'S READING
EMPTY ARMS | CHAPTER ONE | PAGES 11–14

> *There is no greater agony than bearing an untold story inside you.*
> **MAYA ANGELOU**

Your Story

As you begin this journal, I want to ask you to write down all the memories you can recall about your loss. Telling your story is powerful, healing work, not easily confined to the five-step process I'll lead you through in the days to come. So we'll limit today's writing to the memories of your loss and conserve energy to process more later.

As hard as I know it will be, write down the details of the day you lost your baby. Picture the scene and the circumstances and describe them in as much detail as you can. What did you sense, see, hear, taste, touch, smell, and feel? When do you remember thinking that something was wrong? What was your first reaction? How did you feel hours later?

REDUCING PROLONGED GRIEF SYMPTOMS

Studies show that retelling the story of your loss effectively reduces what is referred to by medical specialists as Complicated Grief. [9] Writing the narrative of your loss, including its associations with other life events, its personal significance and meaning to you, and sharing your feelings with supportive others, has been shown to effectively reduce complications of prolonged grief. [10]

My story

The Meaning of My Loss...

Create a visual depiction of how to see the meaning of your loss at this point in your grief process. Use drawings, doodles, clip art, crayons, markers, words, quotes, or whatever helps you capture in picture form what your loss means to you.

THE VALUE OF CREATIVE EXPRESSION

Creative expression can provide a healthy break from grief. Relief comes from being so completely absorbed in an activity that everything else fades into the background.

Brain research shows that activities like music, drawing, meditation, reading, art, crafts, and home projects can stimulate the neurological system and enhance health and well-being. These practices activate the brain's reward system (releasing dopamine), promote the relaxation response, and quiet the body's fight-or-flight response.[11]

DAY TWO
Handling Overwhelming Sadness

TODAY'S READING
EMPTY ARMS | CHAPTER TWO | PAGES 15-22

> *No one ever told me that grief felt so like fear.*
> C.S. LEWIS

Listen To Your Heart

We live in a loud, fast world that leaves our heads swirling with mental noise. Healing requires us to stop moving furiously and to turn off the clamor. To move out of our heads and into our hearts. It's easy to deny or block our feelings when we don't know how to deal with them. But denied feelings don't go away, they go underground. When we bury feelings alive they have a high rate of resurrection, and can overwhelm us later on.

It is common for denial to kick in following a loss. It is a healthy defense mechanism, our primitive and natural defense against pain. But when denial is taken too far, it doesn't serve us well. It blocks us from perceiving the obvious and makes us deaf to important things our hearts have to say to us.

After significant loss, sadness is understandably overwhelming. Journaling is an outlet for processing emotions. It increases self-awareness and emotional intelligence — the ability to perceive and manage our emotions. An effective guard against denial and feeling overwhelmed is to intentionally create a quiet, safe place to listen to what is going on inside, without criticism or judgment. Daily doses of self-awareness can go a long way to keep us moving forward through our grief.

Take some time now to listen to what your heart has to say.

- Using the *Feelings* list on the next page, circle the feelings you experienced while reading chapter two of *Empty Arms* or writing your story on Day One of this journal.

- Draw a double circle around one or two feelings that are most intense or that seem to stay with you longer than others. On a scale of 1-10, with 10 being most intense, identify the level of intensity by writing a number to the right of each feeling you circled.

MISCARRIAGE AND GRIEF

A majority of two hundred and ninety-four women who had experienced a miscarriage said they experienced troublesome feelings of depression, lower self-esteem, self-blame, guilt, and stress in the first year after loss.[12] Normal grief after pregnancy loss includes disbelief, yearning, anger, and depression which are initially high and decline most steeply over the first year. Researchers followed-up with parents to reassess their grief scores 2 years after they lost a baby. 41 % of the parents showed a normal decline of grief scores. 59% showed patterns of prolonged grief and delayed resolution.[13]

TODAY MY HEART IS SAYING...

My Feelings

	HAPPY	SAD	ANGRY	SCARED	ASHAMED
INTENSITY OF FEELINGS	**Excited**	**Depressed**	**Furious**	**Terrified**	**Defamed**
	Overjoyed	**Agonized**	**Enraged**	**Horrified**	**Remorseful**
	Elated	**Alone**	**Outraged**	**Scared stiff**	**Dishonored**
	Thrilled	**Hurt**	**Boiling**	**Fearful**	**Admonished**
	Fired Up	**Sorrowful**	**Irate**	**Panicky**	
		Miserable	**Seething**	**Shocked**	
	Gratified	Heartbroken	Upset	Apprehensive	Apologetic
	Cheerful	Somber	Mad	Frightened	Sneaky
	Satisfied	Lost	Defended	Insecure	Guilty
	Relieved	Distressed	Frustrated	Uneasy	Secretive
	Glowing	Melancholy	Agitated	Intimidated	
		Let Down	Disgusted	Threatened	
	Glad	Unhappy	Perturbed	Nervous	Ridiculous
	Pleasant	Moody	Annoyed	Worried	Regretful
	Tender	Blue	Uptight	Timid	Pitied
	Pleased	Upset	Irritated	Unsure	Silly
	Mellow	Disappointed	Touchy	Anxious	
		Dissatisfied	Resistant	Cautious	

17

The hardest thing today is . . .

_____

It feels risky to . . .

_____

Now create a visual display with drawings, doodles, clip art, crayons, markers, words, quotes, or whatever helps you capture your heart in picture form.

> *Don't even try to be strong. Your tears are a*
> *natural response to your grief. Go ahead and cry.*
>
> JERRY COOK

BENEFITS OF ARTISTIC EXPRESSION

Over a decade of scientific research reveals important benefits of creative expression through art:

- improved well-being, decreased negative emotions and increased positive ones
- improved medical outcomes, reduced depression
- reduced stress and anxiety
- reduced distress
- reduced symptoms of compassion fatigue
- increased healing and sense of purpose
- improved focus on positive life experiences, self-worth, and social identity[14]

My heart looks like this today...

LINGER IN GOD'S LIGHT

Relax and Breathe

Stress is our body's natural reaction to any kind of demand that disrupts life as usual. When we encounter a life-threatening situation, a built-in defense mechanism in our body triggers a surge of stress hormones, preparing us to fight or to flee. As a result, our hearts pound, our muscles tense, our blood pressure rises, and we are suddenly on high alert.[15] This acute stress response is designed to help us survive in the face of danger.

In small doses, stress is good—such as when it helps us to conquer a fear or gives us extra energy to protect ourselves from very real danger. But when it is over-activated, it takes a toll.

Unhealthy stress is often triggered by circumstances that threaten to take away our sense of control. The season of mourning is a highly stressful time of adjustment. We are more easily triggered into fight or flight by non-life-threatening situations because our loss blindsided us. We didn't ask for this. It wasn't our choice. Our natural defenses are weakened and we feel stripped of our sense of control. Hypervigilance kicks in. We scan the radar screen for danger blips in an effort to hang on to what little sense of safety and control we think we have left.

You can optimize your grief recovery by using a number of helpful calming tools, including 3-Dimensional Breathing. Harvard Medical School Professor, Herbert Benson, spearheaded research more than forty years ago on the positive impact of deep breathing and its ability to elicit a relaxation response in the body. This acts as an innate stress buffer.[16] When we engage in controlled deep breathing, our parasympathetic nervous system, which triggers a rest-and-relax response, comes online and counters our sympathetic nervous system's fight-or-flight reaction to threat. Intentional deep breathing stimulates the vagus nerve, which runs from the base of the brain to our abdomen. The vagus nerve mediates our nervous system responses, lowering heart rate, among other things. It also releases a neurotransmitter called acetylcholine that increases focus, and decreases anxiety.[17]

Bouncing back from a devastating loss is best achieved with a relaxed body rather than one that is agitated, continually on guard, anticipating something bad to happen. When grief bears down taxing our resources, our breathing is often shallow and we don't even realize it. A simple way to quickly relax the body is to use 3-D breathing. This fully activates the calming branch of our nervous system.

3-D Breathing is easy to learn. When practiced throughout the day, it can calm the nervous system and pull the body out of a high-alert over-amped state. One way to learn how to belly breathe is to lie on the floor and place a light book on your stomach, and one hand on the side of your waist so that your fingers reach slightly under your lower back. Place your other hand on your upper chest and neck. Fill your lower lungs with air, breathing into your diaphragm, expanding the air equally into the hand that is placed on your side and into your stomach. The book should rise slightly but the hand on your chest should not move. As you breathe out, the book will fall as the air leaves your lungs. 3-D breathing looks like an expanding umbrella: Aim for your midsection to expand in three directions like an umbrella. The hand on your chest rises very little on the last part of your inhale. You don't want to feel your neck contract or tighten.[18]

With practice, you can learn to use 3-D breathing to manage stress reactions on the spot. It's nearly impossible for the body to stay in fight or flight when you intentionally deep breathe. The calming technique is as simple as this:

- Breathe in through your nose to the count of 4.

- Hold your breath to the count of 4.

- Breathe out through your lips to the count of 8.

- Repeat this 4 or more times until you feel your body and mind relax.

Stop now and try it. Take a deep breath in, filling your lungs to capacity. Hold the breath for four seconds, and then exhale very slowly. Notice your body letting go of tension as you breathe out. If you like, add a simple prayer. As you inhale, ask God to fill you afresh with the Holy Spirit. Slowly exhale all the stress into God's care. Repeat this inhale/exhale pattern four times to quiet yourself and improve your ability to focus on what you'll read next.

Read

Invite the Holy Spirit to illumine your mind as you slowly read the following scriptures out loud. Circle words and phrases that resonate with you. Be attentive to thoughts, pictures, and impressions that surface. Don't hurry. Linger and receive.

> You keep track of all my sorrows.
> You have collected all my tears in your bottle.
> You have recorded each one in your book.
> My enemies will retreat when I call to you for help.
> This I know: God is on my side! . . .
> I will fulfill my vows to you, O God,
> and will offer a sacrifice of thanks for your help.
> For you have rescued me from death;
> you have kept my feet from slipping.
> So now I can walk in your presence, O God,
> in your life-giving light.

Psalm 56:8-13, NLT

———————————

Jesus spoke to the people once more and said, "I am the light of the world. If you follow me, you won't have to walk in darkness, because you will have the light that leads to life."

John 8:12 NLT

May the God of hope fill you with all joy and peace as you trust in him, so that you may overflow with hope by the power of the Holy Spirit.

Romans 15:13 NLT

If you are walking in darkness,
Without a ray of light,
Trust in the LORD
And rely on your God.

Isaiah 50:10 NLT

Reflect

What shines out to you from God's Word? Why, specifically, does it call to you?

Renew

Today I will . . .

I will share what I have chosen to do with . . .

THE POWER OF A WRITTEN CHOICE

A written choice has power. A bundle of nerves at the base of your brain, the RAS (Reticular Activating System), filters up to two million pieces of incoming data at any time from your five senses. When you write down your choices, you signal your brain that "this is important." The RAS then flags relevant options and ways to help you make that choice. More detailed choices create a pattern in your brain that it will more likely revert to later.[19]

Release and Receive

God, today I release denial and pretense. I choose to be honest with myself and with You. I realize that I can't deal with this heartache alone, and release myself from trying to do so. I open my heart to receive Your guidance and power.

LOOK FOR THE GOOD

You find what you look for.

Intense pain has a tendency to distort our perception and magnetize us toward negative ruminations about the past and persistent worries about the future. Stability and peace of mind, however, are realized by living in the moment and noticing the good. We can zero in on what is missing in our lives, or we can focus on what is present. Relief comes when we cultivate the habit of looking for the good. You find what you look for.

In one scientific study, participants were invited to write down three good things that went well, daily, for one week. They were asked to add some detail, including how each good thing made them feel, and why they thought each good thing happened (e.g., a heartfelt thank you from a friend, a quiet moment drinking their favorite beverage, or a child's infectious laughter). After one week of this daily activity the participants acknowledged feeling happier and less depressed than when they started. They also maintained this emotional boost six month later, revealing the powerful impact of choosing to look for the good.[20]

Notice three good things that recently went well. How did each make you feel?

1. _____

2. _____

3. _____

What part did you play in those things coming to pass?

1. _____

2. _____

3. _____

LIFT UP THANKS

God gave you a gift of 86,400 seconds today.
Have you used one to say "thank you?"

WILLIAM ARTHUR WARD

A group of Chinese researchers recently studied the combined effects of gratitude and sleep quality on symptoms of anxiety and depression. They found that higher levels of gratitude were associated with better sleep and with lower levels of depression.[21]

Is it any wonder that giving thanks is one of the few specific things that God encourages us to weave through everything in our lives? "in everything give thanks," the Apostle Paul wrote, "for this is God's will for you in Christ Jesus (1 Thessalonians 5:18, NASB).

The primary Hebrew word in the Old Testament that translates to our word *thanks* is *ydh*. It is used seventy-two times and means acknowledging what is right about God in praise and thanksgiving. The Hebrew definition of being thankful is tied entirely to who God is and what He does.

Thankfulness is referenced seventy-one times in the New Testament, and in most instances uses the Greek word *eucharisteo* or a word related to it. *Eucharisteo* means to show oneself grateful, to be thankful, to give thanks, with or without reference to God.[22]

All this talk about definitions is helpful only if we have a means for applying it. We do, so let's do.

> O give thanks to the LORD, for He is good;
> For His lovingkindness is everlasting.
>
> 1 CHRONICLES 16:34

Today I am thankful for . . .

- _____
- _____
- _____

BONUS VIDEO
Morning TV Talk Show Interview - Feeling Is Healing
https://youtu.be/hDnfSwIlREU

THANKFULNESS AND INNER PEACE

Researchers found that the electromagnetic heart patterns of participants became more coherent and ordered when they activated feelings of appreciation. When we think about someone or something we truly appreciate, and experience the feeling that goes with the thought, we trigger the calming branch of the autonomic nervous system. With repetition, this pattern creates a protective effect on the heart. When our hearts are in an "internal coherence state," we enjoy the capacity to be peaceful and calm and yet retain the ability to respond appropriately to stressful circumstances.[23]

LIGHTEN YOUR LOAD

It's time to give yourself permission . . . a lot of it! Let yourself reduce expectations and shift into healing mode. This is not a time for high productivity and achievement. The season of loss is a time to conserve your energy so that your mind and body can heal. Like walking too soon on a broken leg, expecting yourself to do everything you did before your loss can slow healing and complicate recovery.

Today I give myself permission to reduce my expectations and lighten my load. I let go of . . .

_____

_____

_____

_____

_____

DAY THREE
Embracing Your Feelings

TODAY'S READING
EMPTY ARMS | CHAPTER THREE | PAGES 23-30

I thought I could describe a state; make a map of sorrow.
Sorrow, however, turns out to be not a state but a process.

C.S. LEWIS

Listen To Your Heart

"Spinning crazy in endless waves of
unpredictable emotion, it's hard to breathe."

I remember writing those words shortly after our baby died. Flooded with feelings, I wondered how I'd ever get back to experiencing peace in my own skin. Along the way I learned to tune in, to allow the waves to come without despising them, and to ride them out.

God didn't give us feelings to push down, split off, or cast out. Feelings are a gift, and a reflection of being created in God's image. With proper care and attention, emotions tell us what matters and empower us to more fully engage in love and life.

Feeling is healing.

EXPRESSIVE WRITING HELPS POSTPARTUM DEPRESSION AND POST-TRAUMA STRESS

Researchers studied the impact of Expressive Writing on depression and Post-Traumatic Stress symptoms with 113 women after childbirth. Measures were taken three times: the first days after childbirth, then two and three months later. Women participated either an expressive writing group that shared their deep thoughts and feelings, or a neutral writing group that wrote about events of the day. Three months after birth, depressive and Post-Traumatic symptoms were lower for women who used expressive writing, than for those who used neutral writing. Expressive writing was also linked significantly to reductions of Post-Traumatic Stress symptoms at all levels of baseline PTSD, demonstrating the power of expressive writing to reduce postpartum distress.[24]

Take some time now to listen to what your heart has to say.

- Using the *Feelings* list on the next page, circle the feelings you experienced while reading chapter three of *Empty Arms*.

- Draw a double circle around one or two feelings that are most intense or that seem to stay with you longer than others. On a scale of 1-10, with 10 being most intense, identify the level of intensity by writing a number to the right of each feeling you circled.

TODAY MY HEART IS SAYING...

My Feelings

INTENSITY OF FEELINGS

HAPPY	SAD	ANGRY	SCARED	ASHAMED
Excited	**Depressed**	**Furious**	**Terrified**	**Defamed**
Overjoyed	**Agonized**	**Enraged**	**Horrified**	**Remorseful**
Elated	**Alone**	**Outraged**	**Scared stiff**	**Dishonored**
Thrilled	**Hurt**	**Boiling**	**Fearful**	**Admonished**
Fired Up	**Sorrowful**	**Irate**	**Panicky**	
	Miserable	**Seething**	**Shocked**	
Gratified	Heartbroken	Upset	Apprehensive	Apologetic
Cheerful	Somber	Mad	Frightened	Sneaky
Satisfied	Lost	Defended	Insecure	Guilty
Relieved	Distressed	Frustrated	Uneasy	Secretive
Glowing	Melancholy	Agitated	Intimidated	
	Let Down	Disgusted	Threatened	
Glad	Unhappy	Perturbed	Nervous	Ridiculous
Pleasant	Moody	Annoyed	Worried	Regretful
Tender	Blue	Uptight	Timid	Pitied
Pleased	Upset	Irritated	Unsure	Silly
Mellow	Disappointed	Touchy	Anxious	
	Dissatisfied	Resistant	Cautious	

> *That which tears open our souls, those holes that splatter our sight,*
> *may actually become the thin, open places to see through the mess*
> *of this place to the heart-aching beauty beyond.*
> *To Him. To the God whom we endlessly crave.*
>
> ANN VOSKAMP

Relax and Breathe

Sit with both feet on the floor and your hands comfortably on your lap. Close your eyes and breathe in slowly over the course of four seconds, filling your lungs as fully as possible. As you breathe in, invite the Holy Spirit to fill you with life-giving energy and peace. Hold your breath for four seconds, and then slowly exhale. With your exhale, release all stress and nagging thoughts to God, allowing Him to take care of things for the time being.

> *We are mirrors whose brightness is wholly derived*
> *from the sun that shines upon us.*
>
> CS LEWIS

Read

Invite the Holy Spirit to illumine your mind as you slowly read the following scripture passage out loud. Circle words and phrases that resonate with you. Be attentive to thoughts, pictures, and impressions that surface. Don't hurry. Linger and receive.

When Jesus arrived at Bethany, he was told that Lazarus had already been in his grave for four days. Bethany was only a few miles down the road from Jerusalem, and many of the people had come to console Martha and Mary in their loss. When

Martha got word that Jesus was coming, she went to meet him. But Mary stayed in the house. Martha said to Jesus, "Lord, if only you had been here, my brother would not have died. But even now I know that God will give you whatever you ask."

Jesus told her, "Your brother will rise again."

"Yes," Martha said, "he will rise when everyone else rises, at the last day."

Jesus told her, "I am the resurrection and the life. Anyone who believes in me will live, even after dying. Everyone who lives in me and believes in me will never ever die. Do you believe this, Martha?"

"Yes, Lord," she told him. "I have always believed you are the Messiah, the Son of God, the one who has come into the world from God." Then she returned to Mary. She called Mary aside from the mourners and told her, "The Teacher is here and wants to see you." So Mary immediately went to him. Jesus had stayed outside the village, at the place where Martha met him. When the people who were at the house consoling Mary saw her leave so hastily, they assumed she was going to Lazarus's grave to weep. So they followed her there. When Mary arrived and saw Jesus, she fell at his feet and said, "Lord, if only you had been here, my brother would not have died."

When Jesus saw her weeping and saw the other people wailing with her, a deep anger welled up within him, and he was deeply troubled. "Where have you put him?" he asked them.

They told him, "Lord, come and see." Then Jesus wept. The people who were standing nearby said, "See how much he loved him!" But some said, "This man healed a blind man. Couldn't he have kept Lazarus from dying?"

Jesus was still angry as he arrived at the tomb, a cave with a stone rolled across its entrance. "Roll the stone aside," Jesus told them.

But Martha, the dead man's sister, protested, "Lord, he has been dead for four days. The smell will be terrible."

Jesus responded, "Didn't I tell you that you would see God's glory if you believe?" So they rolled the stone aside. Then Jesus looked up to heaven and said, "Father, thank you for hearing me. You always hear me, but I said it out loud for the sake of all these people standing here, so that they will believe you sent me." Then Jesus shouted, "Lazarus, come out!" And the dead man came out, his hands and feet bound in graveclothes, his face wrapped in a headcloth. Jesus told them, "Unwrap him and let him go!"

John 11:17-44 NLT

Reflect

What in the above passage shines out to you? Why?

_____

Renew

Today I will . . . .

_____

Release and Receive

God, today I choose to believe that You are the resurrection and the life. You know the whole picture and have good plans for me. I release my sadness to You and receive Your healing energy into the dead places in my soul.

LOOK FOR THE GOOD

> *Even when it's hard to move, take small steps forward. . .*
> *Every step will lead you further away from where you were*
> *yesterday.*
>
> ANONYMOUS

Stability and peace of mind come from living in the moment and noticing the good. We can focus on what is missing in our lives, or on the good that is present.

Notice three good things that recently went well. How did each make you feel?

1. _____

2. _____

3. _____

What part did you play in those things coming to pass?

1. _____

2. _____

3. _____

LIFT UP THANKS

Levels of gratitude and well-being were measured under three different conditions. People were divided into three groups: One group was asked to journal about negative events or hassles, a second group about the things for which they were grateful, and a third group about neutral life events. People agreed to write in a journal either daily or weekly. Across the three groups, the gratitude group consistently showed evidence of higher well-being scores in comparison with the other two study groups.[25]

Give thanks to the God of heaven.
His faithful love endures forever.

PSALM 136:26

I am thankful that my loss does not define me. It is one piece of the pie, not the whole pie.

I am also thankful for . . .

- _____

- _____

- _____

LIGHTEN YOUR LOAD

Many people feel so pressured by the expectations of others
that it causes them to be frustrated, miserable and confused . . .
But there is a way to live a simple, joy-filled, peaceful life, and
the key is learning how to be led by the Holy Spirit,
not the traditions or expectations of man.

JOYCE MEYER

Today I give myself permission to have realistic expectations. I will let go of . . .

_____

_____

_____

_____

PREVENTING PROLONGED GRIEF COMPLICATIONS

Researchers studied the impact of brief therapy on 228 women who suffered a pregnancy loss. The Treatment Group received Internet counseling for five weeks to help them with self-confrontation, restructuring their thoughts, and social sharing. The Control Group did not receive counseling. Five weeks of counseling was offered to the Control Group following the study. The Treatment Group showed significantly reduced symptoms of posttraumatic stress, prolonged grief, depression, and anxiety relative to the Control Group. Further significant improvement in all PTSD symptoms and prolonged grief was found in post-treatment evaluation at the twelve-month follow-up.[26]

BONUS VIDEO
Paul Young, Author of *The Shack*, and I talk about elements of Good Grief
https://youtu.be/FI_NnP7_wyc

DAY FOUR
Managing Your Anger

TODAY'S READING
EMPTY ARMS | CHAPTER FOUR | PAGES 31 – 36

> *Loss ignites an extraordinary awakening*
> *of the heart to what matters.*

Listen To Your Heart

After losing a baby you experience a wild array of confusing feelings and physical symptoms. Rest assured, you are not losing your mind. Life has abruptly plucked you from your previous familiar world and thrown you into a foreign place you didn't sign up to visit. Anger is a normal response, part of your hardwiring. It is also part of God's original design, and a necessary part of how you are created.

Like a sharp kitchen knife, anger is not inherently destructive. It's a God-given emotion that has a function. It can be helpful or harmful, depending on how we use it. God gives us permission to be angry saying, "Be angry and do not sin."[27] What we do with our anger is what counts.

After pregnancy loss it's common to feel like our body, life, or God has betrayed us. It's understandable to feel angry. Being hard on yourself for feeling angry will only intensify your agitation, entangling you in a cycle of shame and negative preoccupations. However, persistently dwelling in frustration and anger will wreak havoc on your physical and mental health.

Your heart needs extra tender loving care after loss. Brain research shows that thinking compassionately toward yourself decreases muscle tension and heart rate and increases positive emotion, feelings of control, and overall well-being. You can make healthy choices about how you process your loss.[28] Emotional healing progresses by pausing, turning toward your feelings (rather than running away, glossing over, or ignoring them), and acknowledging them with compassion. Simply acknowledge *what is*, without judgment or criticism.

> *When people ask you, "Am I right to be angry?"*
> *Have you thought of asking them, "Am I right to be thirsty?"*
>
> THEODORE ISAAC RUBIN

What color are your feelings?

Color this picture in whatever colors represent your feelings today.

THE IMPACT OF SUPPRESSING AND AVOIDING ON HEALING GRIEF

Scientists interviewed 282 adults who had experienced a significant loss approximately eighteen months prior to a study. Results showed that increased rumination perpetuates symptoms of Complicated Grief. Negative rumination is linked with avoidance and suppression (an individual avoids thinking or talking about their loss, puts off tasks for fear of the potential emotional impact, or avoids acknowledging and dealing with painful emotions). Avoidance complicates grief. Results suggests that those suffering with prolonged grief and chronic rumination may benefit from learning how to counter avoidance and suppression.[29.]

Nothing in this journal can remove the pain you are feeling. Nothing anyone does or says will make the hurt go away. But daily caring for your heart is essential to healing. You are intentionally showing up and being present to honor your love and loss. Now it's time to make space and kindly tend to your heart. Take some time now to listen to what your heart has to say.

- Using the *Feelings* list on the next page, circle the feelings you experienced while reading chapter four of *Empty Arms*.

- Draw a double circle around one or two feelings that are most intense or that seem to stay with you longer than others. On a scale of 1-10, with 10 being most intense, identify the level of intensity by writing a number to the right of each feeling you circled.

TODAY MY HEART IS SAYING...

My Feelings

HAPPY	SAD	ANGRY	SCARED	ASHAMED
Excited	**Depressed**	**Furious**	**Terrified**	**Defamed**
Overjoyed	**Agonized**	**Enraged**	**Horrified**	**Remorseful**
Elated	**Alone**	**Outraged**	**Scared stiff**	**Dishonored**
Thrilled	**Hurt**	**Boiling**	**Fearful**	**Admonished**
Fired Up	**Sorrowful**	**Irate**	**Panicky**	
	Miserable	**Seething**	**Shocked**	
Gratified	Heartbroken	Upset	Apprehensive	Apologetic
Cheerful	Somber	Mad	Frightened	Sneaky
Satisfied	Lost	Defended	Insecure	Guilty
Relieved	Distressed	Frustrated	Uneasy	Secretive
Glowing	Melancholy	Agitated	Intimidated	
	Let Down	Disgusted	Threatened	
Glad	Unhappy	Perturbed	Nervous	Ridiculous
Pleasant	Moody	Annoyed	Worried	Regretful
Tender	Blue	Uptight	Timid	Pitied
Pleased	Upset	Irritated	Unsure	Silly
Mellow	Disappointed	Touchy	Anxious	
	Dissatisfied	Resistant	Cautious	

INTENSITY OF FEELINGS

I feel most angry about . . .

_____

It doesn't seem fair that . . .

_____

The hardest thing about feeling angry is . . .

_____

A good thing about anger is . . .

_____

Draw a symbol of compassion holding your anger.

LINGER IN GOD'S LIGHT

Relax and Breathe

Inhale deeply, filling your lungs to capacity. Hold your breath for four seconds, then exhale very slowly. Notice the physical sensations of the air entering and exiting your body, the air passing through your nose. Feel the relief of letting go of tension as you exhale. With each breath, invite God's love and life-giving energy to refresh you. Exhale your frustrations and stress to God. Repeat this inhale/exhale pattern four times to quiet yourself and prepare to receive from God. Repeat this inhale/exhale pattern four times to quiet yourself and prepare to receive from God.

Read

Invite the Holy Spirit to illumine your mind as you slowly read the following scriptures out loud. Circle words and phrases that resonate with you. Be attentive to thoughts, pictures, and impressions that surface. Don't hurry. Linger and receive.

[Jesus said,] "Are you tired? Worn out?
Burned out on religion?
Come to me. Get away with me and
you'll recover your life.
 I'll show you how to take a real rest.
Walk with me and work with me—watch how I do it.
Learn the unforced rhythms of grace.
I won't lay anything heavy or ill-fitting on you.
Keep company with me and you'll learn to
live freely and lightly."

Matthew 11:28-30 MSG

———————

So, no matter what I say, what I believe, and what I do,
I'm bankrupt without love.
Love never gives up.
Love cares more for others than for self.
Love doesn't want what it doesn't have.
Love doesn't strut,
Doesn't have a swelled head,
Doesn't force itself on others,
Isn't always "Me first,"
Doesn't fly off the handle,
Doesn't keep score of the sins of others,
Doesn't revel when others grovel,
Takes pleasure in the flowering of truth,
Puts up with anything,
Trusts God always,
Always looks for the best,
Never looks back,
But keeps going to the end.
 Love never dies.

1 Corinthians 13:7-10 MSG

Reflect

What in the passages above shines out to you? Why?

_____

Renew

Today I will love myself well by. . .

_____

I will share love with another by . . .

_____

Release and Receive

Lord, today I release . . .

_____

And I open my heart to receive from You . . .

_____

LOOK FOR THE GOOD

> *As my sufferings mounted I soon realized that there were two ways*
> *in which I could respond to my situation -- either to react with*
> *bitterness or seek to transform the suffering into a creative force. I*
> *decided to follow the latter course.*
>
> MARTIN LUTHER KING, JR.

Life after loss weighs heavy and seems void of inspiration. Grief tends to draw us in and away from others, making it easy to forget the magnificence that exists outside our pain. Proactively reversing this tendency by opening our eyes to the wonders around us, gives us a break from negative preoccupations and promotes healing.

Recent research indicates that a small dose of *awe,* that positive goose-bumpy feeling of being in the presence of something vast that transcends us, can go a long way in lifting our spirits and boosting resiliency. It's a powerful way to cut through grief and help us see things in a new light. Awe lifts us outside of our usual routine and opens up fresh new perspective, which can be especially helpful when we're feeling bogged down by day-after-day grief.

In a recent study, one group of people stood in a spectacular grove of towering blue gum eucalyptus trees, some exceeding 200 feet. They gazed up at the trees for one minute, while a second group looked at a building. Those who studied the trees reported greater feelings of awe and a sense of smallness that made everyday concerns seem less overwhelming. They also felt less entitled and were more likely to help someone in need. A simple way to weave awe into your daily routine is to take an Awe Walk. Select a location and approach it with new eyes. You might stroll around your back yard, a nature trail, an art museum, a nearby park, or a garden.[30]

Be intentional about getting out of your head and into the beauty around you. Notice the singing birds, the color and movement in the trees, the sky peeking through foliage high above you, patterns of the clouds and wind, ripples on water, lights twinkling in the dark. Make an effort to notice the good, lovely, and beautiful sights and sounds. God has showered us with these good gifts to fully enjoy. Pausing in awe and thanking God for the little details you notice can bring relief in the midst of grief.[31]

Carve out ten minutes to take an Awe Walk. Once you've done so, list three good things you observed and the feelings you experienced.

1. _____

2. _____

3. _____

Lift Up Thanks

Today I am thankful for . . .

• _____

- _____

- _____

LIGHTEN YOUR LOAD

Just as it is impossible to explain childbirth to a woman who has never given birth, it is impossible to explain child loss to a person who has never lost a child.

LYNDA CHELDELIN FELL

Recent scientific research shows the benefits of being compassionate with yourself and putting it in writing. In one study, people who wrote a self-compassionate letter every day for a week reported less depression and greater happiness three months later than they had beforehand. Their increase in happiness persisted six months later.[32]

It's time to give yourself grace. Write a compassionate note to yourself acknowledging the many ways you are courageously persevering through this season of suffering.

NOTE TO SELF . . . _____

_____

_____

_____

TODAY I LET GO OF . . . _____

_____

_____

_____

DAY FIVE
Untying Guilt's Knot

TODAY'S READING
EMPTY ARMS CHAPTER FIVE: PAGES 37–46

> *Grief is not as heavy as guilt, but it takes more away from you.*
> **VERONICA ROTH**

BONUS VIDEO

Katie Ebner Harman, Miss America 2002, and I talk
live about guilt and shame.
https://youtu.be/fU1ouOzHx10

Listen To Your Heart

You are learning to pay attention to the feelings of your heart, a very important part of who you are and how you are designed. Birds fly. Fish swim. People feel. You've been acknowledging and naming your feelings. When you can name them, you can tame them. Feeling is healing. Take some time now to listen to what your heart has to say.

- Using the *Feelings* list on the next page, circle the feelings you experienced while reading chapter five of *Empty Arms*.

- Draw a double circle around one or two feelings that are most intense or that seem to stay with you longer than others. On a scale of 1-10, with 10 being most intense, identify the level of intensity by writing a number to the right of each feeling you circled.

TODAY MY HEART IS SAYING...

My Feelings

INTENSITY OF FEELINGS

HAPPY	SAD	ANGRY	SCARED	ASHAMED
Excited	**Depressed**	**Furious**	**Terrified**	**Defamed**
Overjoyed	**Agonized**	**Enraged**	**Horrified**	**Remorseful**
Elated	**Alone**	**Outraged**	**Scared stiff**	**Dishonored**
Thrilled	**Hurt**	**Boiling**	**Fearful**	**Admonished**
Fired Up	**Sorrowful**	**Irate**	**Panicky**	
	Miserable	**Seething**	**Shocked**	
Gratified	Heartbroken	Upset	Apprehensive	Apologetic
Cheerful	Somber	Mad	Frightened	Sneaky
Satisfied	Lost	Defended	Insecure	Guilty
Relieved	Distressed	Frustrated	Uneasy	Secretive
Glowing	Melancholy	Agitated	Intimidated	
	Let Down	Disgusted	Threatened	
Glad	Unhappy	Perturbed	Nervous	Ridiculous
Pleasant	Moody	Annoyed	Worried	Regretful
Tender	Blue	Uptight	Timid	Pitied
Pleased	Upset	Irritated	Unsure	Silly
Mellow	Disappointed	Touchy	Anxious	
	Dissatisfied	Resistant	Cautious	

Guilt grows from regret. Preoccupations over what you did or didn't do, or speculations about how you might have prevented your baby's death, can make it difficult to heal. Regrets are common following a loss. What do yours sound like?

I wish I had . . .

_____

If only I . . .

_____

I cannot control . . .

_____

I should have . . .

_____

I could not control . . .

_____

SELF-BLAME AND GUILT AFTER PREGNANCY LOSS

Feelings of self-blame and guilt after pregnancy loss are pronounced for both mothers and fathers. Couples can benefit from caring supporters who are sensitive to their tendencies towards self-blame, guilt, and shame, and who can help them find ways to decrease these feelings.[33]

LINGER IN THE LIGHT

Relax and Breathe

Settle into a quiet, comfortable place. Close your eyes and take in a deep breath, slowly, over the course of four seconds. As you breathe in, invite God to permeate you with life-giving energy and peace. Hold your breath for four seconds, and then slowly exhale. Release all stress and nagging thoughts to God, allowing Him to take them for the time being. Repeat this inhale/exhale pattern four times to quiet yourself and prepare to receive from God.

Read

While you read the following scripture passage, expect the Holy Spirit to shine the spotlight on certain ideas. Be attentive to the thoughts, pictures, and impressions that come to you. Feel free to circle words and phrases that resonate with you. Don't hurry. This is your time to linger in God's presence and receive what you need.

> *Like the wind, Grace finds us wherever we are*
> *And won't leave us however we were found.*
>
> ANN VOSKAMP

But let me tell you something wonderful, a mystery I'll probably never fully understand. We're not all going to die—*but* we are all going to be changed. You hear a blast to end all blasts from a trumpet, and in the time that you look up and blink your eyes—it's over. On signal from that trumpet from heaven, the dead will be up and out of their graves, beyond the reach of death, never to die again. At the same moment and in the same way, we'll all be changed. In the resurrection scheme of things, this has to happen: everything perishable taken off the shelves and replaced by the imperishable, this mortal replaced by the immortal. Then the saying will come true: Death swallowed by triumphant Life! Who got the last word, oh, Death? Oh, Death, who's afraid of you now? It was sin that made death so frightening and law-code guilt that gave sin its leverage, its destructive power. But now in a single victorious stroke of Life, all three—sin, guilt, death—are gone, the gift of our Master, Jesus Christ. Thank God!

I Cor. 15:51-57, MSG

He (Jesus) came into Sychar, a Samaritan village that bordered the field Jacob had given his son Joseph. Jacob's well was still there. Jesus, worn out by the trip, sat down at the well. It was noon.

A woman, a Samaritan, came to draw water. Jesus said, "Would you give me a drink of water?" (His disciples had gone to the village to buy food for lunch.) The Samaritan woman, taken aback, asked, "How come you, a Jew, are asking me, a Samaritan woman, for a drink?" (Jews in those days wouldn't be caught dead talking to Samaritans.)

Jesus answered, "If you knew the generosity of God and who I am, you would be asking *me* for a drink, and I would give you fresh, living water."

The woman said, "Sir, you don't even have a bucket to draw with, and this well is deep. So how are you going to get this 'living water'? Are you a better man than our ancestor Jacob, who dug this well and drank from it, he and his sons and livestock, and passed it down to us?"

Jesus said, "Everyone who drinks this water will get thirsty again and again. Anyone who drinks the water I give will never thirst— not ever. The water I give will be an artesian spring within, gushing fountains of endless life.

The woman said, "Sir, give me this water so I won't ever get thirsty, won't ever have to come back to this well again! . . . (Jesus) "The time is coming—it has, in fact, come—when what you're called will not matter and where you go to worship will not matter. It's who you are and the way you live that count before God. Your worship must engage your spirit in the pursuit of truth. That's the kind of people the Father is out looking for: those who are simply and honestly themselves before him in their worship." in their worship. God is sheer being itself—Spirit. Those who worship him must do it out of their very being, their spirits, their true selves, in adoration."

John 4:4-15, 22-24 MSG

Reflect

What in the passage above shines out to you? Why?

_____

Renew

Imagine yourself as the woman in the story. What are your thoughts and feelings after Jesus tells you things about yourself and the bigger picture?

_____

How do you want to act on your insights today?

Today I will . . .

_____

Release and Receive

Lord, I release guilt and regrets to You. I drink in your life-giving water and receive Your power to be kind and gentle with myself. I choose to forgive myself. Wash away the dust of death and anything else clouding my life that is not of You.

> *You can't forgive without loving. And I don't mean sentimentality. I don't mean mush. I mean having enough courage to stand up and say, "I forgive. I'm finished with it."*
>
> MAYA ANGELOU

LOOK FOR THE GOOD

Grief tends to pull our thoughts onto a negative track. We can fall into the trap of thinking too much about what is wrong in our lives and not enough about what is good and right. Looking for the good helps us tune into the everyday sources of pleasure around us, which in turn lifts our emotions in profound ways. Writing down the good things cements them in our awareness, deepening their positive emotional impact.

Several years ago researchers studied the effect on well-being of counting your blessings in daily life. Those who wrote down their blessings once a week for ten weeks, or daily for two or three weeks, experienced more positive moods, optimism about the future, and better sleep than those who did not.[34]

What are the special blessings in your life today?

- _____
- _____
- _____

LIFT UP THANKS

A grateful heart is a magnet for miracles.
ANONYMOUS

Tell God why you are grateful for these three specific blessings:

- _____
- _____
- _____

LIGHTEN YOUR LOAD

This is a season of suffering. It's hard. It's healthy and helpful for you to alternate between embracing your painful thoughts and feelings and taking a time-out from grief. Parents who are grieving often feel guilty for allowing themselves to be distracted from the pain of their loss. They feel guilty about not having a successful pregnancy. They feel guilty about not feeling better faster. Self-criticism tends to go hand in hand with guilt.

Grief is a long process that requires pacing and mental rest along the way. Please allow yourself to take a breather now and then to quiet negative ruminations. Finding ways to meet your need for refreshment and renewal will enhance the quality of your life, and energize you to care for those who rely on you.

THE IMPACT OF MEDITATION ON SELF-CRITICISM AND EMOTIONS

Thirty-eight individuals with high scores on the self-critical perfectionism scale were divided into a Loving Kindness Meditation group or a control group. Measures of self-criticism, self-compassion, and distress were taken before and immediately following the intervention. Scores were gathered again three months after the meditation. Results indicate that loving-kindness meditation is effective in helping self-critical individuals become less self-critical and more self-compassionate. Practicing loving-kindness may also reduce depressive symptoms and increase positive emotions.[35]

A LOVING-KINDNESS MEDITATION
TO LIGHTEN YOUR LOAD

I created this guided meditation based on truths from Scripture to give you an opportunity to soak in God's love. Read through the paragraphs in italics to familiarize yourself with the content. Whenever you are ready, read it out loud, or ask a loved one to read it out loud, and record the prayer below either on your phone or another device. (Some women like to play soft relaxing instrumental music in the background while recording.) Use the recording periodically to give yourself a grief time-out and shut down negative ruminations.

In a comfortable, quiet place, relax and take four slow deep cleansing breaths. With your eyes closed, think of a person who is safe and kind. Someone who loves you. Imagine them sitting close to you on your right. They see the best in you. They believe in you. Feel the warmth of their loving-kindness. They are thankful and happy to be with you.

Now bring to mind the very good Father God, Jesus who gave His life for you, and the Holy Spirit who comforts and guides you. Envision this perfect union of unspoiled love, the One who was, and is, and is to come. Imagine yourself sitting in the center, surrounded on all sides by the divine trinity, immersed in heavenly light. Soak in the warming comfort of God's loving presence. Feel the radiant joy that shines around and upon you. Be mindful of what God says about you as you listen to this interactive prayer:

"You, my precious daughter, are Mine. You are completely accepted. You are totally forgiven. Nothing from your past, present, or future will ever change My love for you. My love always remains steady, constant, and unwavering. Nothing can hinder or remove my love for you.

I am for you. I am in you, beside you, behind you, and in front of you, leading you through this season. You can trust Me to orchestrate the way through. I know where I am going. Simply stay close and follow Me.

Your changing moods and circumstances do not change the fact that you are deeply cherished and fully embraced in My unconditional love. I know you better than you know yourself. You are who you are by divine design. I created you in love for significance and purpose in your world. Trust that I am crafting magnificence in you, mending the torn places of your soul, and breathing resurrection life to everything in you that needs My touch. I am the God who heals and restores.

Be confident that I am always near, dwelling in your heart.
Even when you feel alone, you are not alone.
I am with you in this passing season.
I will bring you through, shining brighter than gold.
You can count on My promise. I will never leave or forsake you.
Know that I am right here, close, always attentive to your voice.
Rest in My grace. Lean into My love.
You are safe here."

Take another deep breath in, filling your lungs, and then relax. Let it go. Just relax and bask in the warmth and kindness of God. Refresh in God's renewing presence. You are filled to overflowing with peace and love.

———————

Now begin sending your love back to God by lifting up thanks . . .

Thank You for taking me as I am and for loving me.

Thank You for sharing the burden of my suffering.

Thank You for taking care of my baby until we meet again.

Thank You for enveloping my baby in Your perfect love, free from pain and sadness.

Thank You for Your promise to bring new life out of death.

Your life is always greater than death.

Thank You for breathing the very essence of Your life force into me, empowering me to choose life—a life continually graced with fresh hope, courage, and strength, by the power of Your Spirit.

Thank You for leading me out of the darkness into the bright open spaces of Your presence. Thank You for lifting me up, holding me close, and carrying me whenever I need it. Thank You for always being near, for noticing my tears, understanding my confusion, and mending my soul. I trust You to orchestrate creative miracles in me today.

Thank You for promising to complete the good work You began in me, and for giving me reasons to smile.

Now take another deep cleansing breath. Linger a moment and be aware of whatever you are sensing.

NOTE TO SELF:

As I soaked in God's love and truth I became aware of . . .

_____

_____

_____

_____

DAY SIX
Overcoming Spiritual Battles

TODAY'S READING
EMPTY ARMS CHAPTER SIX: PAGES 47-52

> *The heart has its reasons of which reason knows nothing.*
> BLAISE PASCAL

Listen To Your Heart

Grief ushers us into strong feelings of loneliness and vulnerability. Our sense of worth and confidence is challenged after losing a baby. We battle with accepting our loss for what it is, our powerlessness to change the outcome, and our inability to quickly feel better on every level – physically, emotionally, and spiritually. This is a time when we need to be more open to receive tender loving compassion from God and others.

Receiving love in relationships, releases the hormone oxytocin, which calms our brain and increases our sense of safety and connection. Studies of brain activity using functional magnetic resonance imaging, show that oxytocin suppresses activity in the part of the brain that processes fear (amygdala). By compassionately recognizing your suffering, loving yourself well, and receiving love from God and others, you prime the brain to be more calm and clear, as well as more trusting and adaptive in this difficult season.[36]

Take some time now to listen to what your heart has to say.

- Using the *Feelings* list on the next page, circle the feelings you experienced while reading chapter six of *Empty Arms*.

- Draw a double circle around one or two feelings that are most intense or that seem to stay with you longer than others. On a scale of 1-10, with 10 being most intense, identify the level of intensity by writing a number to the right of each feeling you circled.

TODAY MY HEART IS SAYING...

My Feelings

HAPPY	SAD	ANGRY	SCARED	ASHAMED
Excited	**Depressed**	**Furious**	**Terrified**	**Defamed**
Overjoyed	**Agonized**	**Enraged**	**Horrified**	**Remorseful**
Elated	**Alone**	**Outraged**	**Scared stiff**	**Dishonored**
Thrilled	**Hurt**	**Boiling**	**Fearful**	**Admonished**
Fired Up	**Sorrowful**	**Irate**	**Panicky**	
	Miserable	**Seething**	**Shocked**	
Gratified	Heartbroken	Upset	Apprehensive	Apologetic
Cheerful	Somber	Mad	Frightened	Sneaky
Satisfied	Lost	Defended	Insecure	Guilty
Relieved	Distressed	Frustrated	Uneasy	Secretive
Glowing	Melancholy	Agitated	Intimidated	
	Let Down	Disgusted	Threatened	
Glad	Unhappy	Perturbed	Nervous	Ridiculous
Pleasant	Moody	Annoyed	Worried	Regretful
Tender	Blue	Uptight	Timid	Pitied
Pleased	Upset	Irritated	Unsure	Silly
Mellow	Disappointed	Touchy	Anxious	
	Dissatisfied	Resistant	Cautious	

INTENSITY OF FEELINGS

LINGER IN GOD'S LIGHT

> *Between a stimulus and a response there is a space. In that space is our power to choose our response. In our response lies our growth and our freedom. The last of human freedoms is to choose one's attitude in any given set of circumstances.*
>
> VIKTOR FRANKL, AUSTRIAN PSYCHIATRIST
> AND SURVIVOR OF AUSCHWITZ

Relax and Breathe

Inhale deeply, filling your lungs to capacity. Hold your breath for four seconds, then exhale very slowly. Notice the physical sensations of the air entering and exiting your body. Feel the relief of letting go of tension as you exhale. With each breath, invite God's love and life-giving energy to refresh you. Exhale your frustrations and stress to God. Repeat this inhale/exhale pattern four times to quiet yourself and prepare to receive from God.

Read

We are living our lives in the context of a spiritual war.[37] Jesus teaches that things work in the spiritual realm in certain ways, just as things in the physical universe work in certain ways. We have absolutely nothing to fear because the victory of Christ on the cross breaks the power of sin and darkness in our lives. God has already won the spiritual war. When we are too weak to fight our own battles, God moves against our enemies for us.[38] The Living God who reigns supreme, is continuously advocating and interceding on our behalf.[39]

Invite the Holy Spirit to illumine your mind as you slowly read the following scriptures out loud. Circle words and phrases that resonate with you. Be attentive to thoughts, pictures, and impressions that surface. Don't hurry. Linger and receive.

...when you pray, go into your room, and when you have shut your door, pray to your Father who *is* in the secret *place;* and your Father who sees in secret will reward you openly. And when you pray, do not use vain repetitions as the heathen *do.* For they think that they will be heard for their many words.

"Therefore do not be like them. For your Father knows the things you have need of before you ask Him. In this manner, therefore, pray:

> Our Father in heaven,
> Hallowed be Your name.
> Your kingdom come.
> Your will be done
> On earth as *it is* in heaven.
> Give us this day our daily bread.
>
> And forgive us our debts,
> As we forgive our debtors.
> And do not lead us into temptation,
> But deliver us from the evil one.
> For Yours is the kingdom and the power and the glory
> forever. Amen.

Matthew 6: 5-13 NKJV

For who is God except the Lord?
Who but our God is a solid rock?
God arms me with strength,
and he makes my way perfect.
He makes me as surefooted as a deer,
enabling me to stand on mountain heights.

He trains my hands for battle;
he strengthens my arm to draw a bronze bow.
You have given me your shield of victory.
Your right hand supports me;
your help has made me great.
You have made a wide path for my feet
to keep them from slipping.
I chased my enemies and caught them;
I did not stop until they were conquered.
I struck them down so they could not get up;
they fell beneath my feet.
You have armed me with strength for the battle;
you have subdued my enemies under my feet.

Psalm 18:30-39 NLT

Be self-controlled and alert. Your enemy the devil prowls around like a roaring lion looking for someone to devour. Resist him, standing firm in the faith, because you know that your brothers throughout the world are undergoing the same kind of sufferings.

1 Peter 5:8-9 NLT

Reflect

What words, phrases, or ideas shine out to you? Why?

_____

Renew

Today I will . . .

_____

I will share one of my insights with. . .

_____

Release and Receive

Lord, today I release to You . . .

_____

I open my heart to receive from You . . .

_____

> *...when you and I approach God for help, filled with our cares and distresses, our prayers are not confined to this calendar date, to this particular month and year. What may seem to be His silence and avoidance from where you sit today, is already reverberating in future places. If not right here, if not right now, you can be sure His ability is taking visible, tangible shape somewhere, even if beyond the scope of your current sightline.*
>
> PRISCILLA SHIRER

LOOK FOR THE GOOD

When our stress levels are up following a significant loss, we tend to hunt for ways to escape. We also tend to over-focus on negatives, including personal flaws. Overwhelmed by grief, our weaknesses loom large. Automatic Negative Thoughts (ANTS) take center stage, making it easy to forget the good about ourselves, our spiritual resources, and our strength in God.

To counter this negative tendency, consider your character strengths and spiritual assets such as creativity, kindness, vitality, faith, trust, perseverance, wisdom, courage, self-control, relational sensitivity, thoughtfulness, gratitude, and love.

If something comes easily to you, you may take it for granted and not identify it as a strength. If you are not sure of your assets, you can identify them by asking someone you respect who knows you well, by noticing how people compliment you, and by thinking about what comes most easily to you. Certain strengths are most closely linked to happiness, gratitude, hope, zest, curiosity, and love. These strengths are worth cultivating and using daily, even if they don't come naturally to you.[40]

RELIEF IN SUFFERING

Researchers tested five different interventions with severely depressed patients. They found that the Use Your Strengths exercise increased happiness and decreased depressive symptoms, and that that happiness boost lasted up to six months. They suggested the potential use of this exercise in connection with traditional treatments that relieve suffering.[41]

List seven of your inner strengths:

1. _____

2. _____

3. _____

4. _____

5. _____

6. _____

7. _____

Select a strength and make a plan to use it each day this week. You can practice the same strength each day, or choose a different one. Afterward, write about what you did, how it made you feel, and what you learned.

Select one strength from your list above and write down how you will express it today.

Today I will . . .

_____

Afterward, record the results.

I used my strength today by . . .

_____

Using my strength makes me feel . . .

_____

I learned . . .

_____

> *I do not at all understand the mystery of grace — only that it meets us where we are but does not leave us where it found us.*
>
> ANNE LAMOTT

LIFT UP THANKS

> *The Lord is a shelter for the oppressed, a refuge in times of trouble.*
> *Those who know your name trust in you,*
> *For you, O Lord, do not abandon those who search for you.*
>
> PSALM 9:9-10 NLT

Today I am thankful for . . .

- _____
- _____
- _____

One way to lighten our load is to simply use the weapons and authority God has given us and, in faith, declare victory over dark influences. Below is a sample warfare prayer that can be used to establish victory over darkness.

A Victory Declaration

"Lord Jesus Christ, Son of the Living God, You are my Savior. Thank You for paying for my sins with Your own blood when You chose to lay down Your life for me.[42] Thank You for Your great love for me, for being so rich in mercy, and for saving me by Your grace.[43] My life belongs to You and to no one else.[44] Satan has no claim on me. Open the eyes of my heart to more fully understand the authority You have given to me as Your daughter. By faith, I declare that I am victorious over all the powers of darkness because You disarmed all the spiritual dark powers and authorities when You triumphed over them on the cross.[45] Jesus, You destroyed the power of death held by the devil, and You freed me from the chains of darkness.[46] I declare that God has not given me a spirit of fear, but a spirit of power, love, and a sound mind.[47]

I command the spirit of fear to go where Jesus Christ commands it to go, and to never return. All fear is defeated by the shed blood of Jesus. I break agreement with all unhealthy worry, anxiety, and anger. I take back any ground where the devil has had influence in my life.[48] He is no longer permitted to trespass. I break agreement with all the lies of the enemy, and all resulting confusion, in Jesus' name. With the authority God has given me to overcome all the power of the enemy, I establish my victory right here and right now.[49] Lord Jesus, I present myself to You once again, in full surrender. I submit to You, resist the devil, and by faith agree with You that his influence is now defeated. I ask You Lord to please heal, restore, and make me whole. As I go forward, show me how I can cooperate with You in the healing process.

In the mighty name of the Lord Jesus Christ, King of Kings and Lord of Heaven's armies. Amen."

Today I let go of . . .

_____

_____

_____

_____

_____

_____

The enemy always tries to keep you from praying against him, as Jesus taught us to pray, because he knows once you learn how to do this, his gig is up.

JOHN ELDREDGE

DAY SEVEN
Responding to the Actions of Others – Part One

TODAY'S READING
EMPTY ARMS | CHAPTER SEVEN | PAGES 53–60

> *The death of a baby is like a stone cast into the stillness of a quiet pool; the concentric ripples of despair sweep out in all directions, affecting many, many people.*
>
> JOHN DEFRAIN

Listen To Your Heart

Unresolved grief is like a windshield smeared with thick mud. It prevents us from seeing clearly and moving forward on the road ahead.

You've chosen to proactively engage in *good grief* by committing twenty-one days to explore your heart, paying attention to what is often ignored, and productively processing your heartache. This says volumes about your desire to heal and your determination to take responsibility for your well-being. Listening to your heart allows you to more thoroughly comprehend the layered meaning of your love and loss and to partner with God in your healing process.

THE BENEFITS OF JOURNALING

- clarify your thoughts and feelings
- know yourself better
- reduce stress
- solve problems more effectively
- resolve disagreements with others.[50]

Emotional healing progresses by pausing, facing your feelings, and turning toward God. There is no need to hide, or to shy away from the pain. God is with you. You are safe in His presence. He fully embraces you as you are and compassionately waits to be invited into the wounded places of your soul. Jesus loves to explore the deeper places of your heart with you, to make Himself known to you, and to heal you. He sees everything and understands your feelings better than you do.

Take some time now to listen to what your heart has to say.

- Using the *Feelings* list on the next page, circle the feelings you experienced while reading the first part of chapter seven in *Empty Arms*.

- Draw a double circle around one or two feelings that are most intense or that seem to stay with you longer than others. On a scale of 1-10, with 10 being most intense, identify the level of intensity by writing a number to the right of each feeling you circled.

What color are your feelings?

Color this picture in whatever colors represent your feelings today.

TODAY MY HEART IS SAYING...

My Feelings

HAPPY	SAD	ANGRY	SCARED	ASHAMED
Excited	**Depressed**	**Furious**	**Terrified**	**Defamed**
Overjoyed	**Agonized**	**Enraged**	**Horrified**	**Remorseful**
Elated	**Alone**	**Outraged**	**Scared stiff**	**Dishonored**
Thrilled	**Hurt**	**Boiling**	**Fearful**	**Admonished**
Fired Up	**Sorrowful**	**Irate**	**Panicky**	
	Miserable	**Seething**	**Shocked**	
Gratified	Heartbroken	Upset	Apprehensive	Apologetic
Cheerful	Somber	Mad	Frightened	Sneaky
Satisfied	Lost	Defended	Insecure	Guilty
Relieved	Distressed	Frustrated	Uneasy	Secretive
Glowing	Melancholy	Agitated	Intimidated	
	Let Down	Disgusted	Threatened	
Glad	Unhappy	Perturbed	Nervous	Ridiculous
Pleasant	Moody	Annoyed	Worried	Regretful
Tender	Blue	Uptight	Timid	Pitied
Pleased	Upset	Irritated	Unsure	Silly
Mellow	Disappointed	Touchy	Anxious	
	Dissatisfied	Resistant	Cautious	

INTENSITY OF FEELINGS

Think about the ways various people have responded to your loss. Record responses that increased your heartache.

It was hard for me when_____ said/did . . .

_____

What feeling words are connected with this experience?

_____

It was hard for me when_____ didn't . . .

_____

What feeling words are connected with this experience?

_____

Now record responses that eased your heartache:

_____

It helped me when _____ said/did . . .

_____

What feeling words are connected with this experience?

_____

It helped me when _____ didn't . . .

_____

What feeling words are connected with this experience?

_____

We learn best how to effectively care for others who are suffering by being on the receiving end of wise and loving compassion. Who has been a tangible source of comfort for you during this time of grief?

LINGER IN GOD'S LIGHT

> *The friend who can be silent with us in a moment of despair*
> *or confusion, who can stay with us in an hour of grief and*
> *bereavement, who can tolerate not knowing . . . not healing, not*
> *curing . . . that is a friend who cares.*
>
> HENRI NOUWEN

When we slow down and linger with Jesus, He empowers us to relax and accept ourselves as He does, perfectly and completely, with all of our strengths and imperfections. We begin to better understand experientially what it means to enter the rest of His unconditional love. There's no better time to step into that place called peace, than right now.

Relax and Breathe

Inhale deeply, filling your lungs to capacity. Hold your breath for four seconds, then exhale very slowly. Notice the physical sensations of the air entering and exiting your body. Feel the relief of letting go of tension as you exhale. With each breath, invite the God Almighty, who gave you life, to fill you afresh with His Spirit. Exhale your frustrations and stress to God. Repeat this inhale/exhale pattern four times to quiet yourself and prepare to receive from God.

Read

When we enter God's presence, He shows us things to encourage and refresh our souls. He knows our needs better than we do, and promises to meet us where we are, and to lead us forward into solutions. The greater our problems, the greater His provision. Invite the Holy Spirit to illumine your mind as you slowly read the following scriptures out loud. Circle words and phrases that resonate with you. Be attentive to thoughts, pictures, and impressions that surface. Don't hurry. Linger and receive.

JESUS PRAYS IN GETHSEMANE…

Then Jesus went with them to the olive grove called Gethsemane, and he said, "Sit here while I go over there to pray." He took Peter and Zebedee's two sons, James and John, and he became anguished and distressed. He told them, "My soul is crushed with grief to the point of death. Stay here and keep watch with me."

He went on a little farther and bowed with his face to the ground, praying, "My Father! If it is possible, let this cup of suffering be taken away from me. Yet I want your will to be done, not mine."

Then he returned to the disciples and found them asleep. He said to Peter, "Couldn't you watch with me even one hour? Keep watch and pray, so that you will not give in to temptation. For the spirit is willing, but the body is weak!"

Then Jesus left them a second time and prayed, "My Father! If this cup cannot be taken away unless I drink it, your will be done." When he returned to them again, he found them sleeping, for they couldn't keep their eyes open.

So he went to pray a third time, saying the same things again. Then he came to the disciples and said, "Go ahead and sleep. Have your rest. But look—the time has come. The Son of Man is betrayed into the hands of sinners. Up, let's be going. Look, my betrayer is here!"

Matthew 26:36-44 NLT

JESUS ANNOUNCES HIS PURPOSE FOR COMING TO THIS WORLD…

The Spirit of the Sovereign Lord is on me,
Because the Lord has anointed me to proclaim good news to the poor.
He has sent me to bind up the brokenhearted,

To proclaim freedom for the captives
And release from darkness for the prisoners,
To proclaim the year of the Lord's favor
And the day of vengeance of our God, to comfort all who mourn,
And provide for those who grieve . . .to bestow on them
A crown of beauty instead of ashes, the oil of joy instead of
mourning, And the garment of praise instead of a spirit of despair.

Luke 4:18-19; Isaiah 61:1-3 NIV

While Jesus was here on earth, he offered prayers and pleadings,
with a loud cry and tears, to the one who could rescue him from
death. And God heard his prayers because of his deep reverence
for God. Even though Jesus was God's Son, he learned obedience
from the things he suffered. In this way, God qualified him as a
perfect High Priest, and he became the source of eternal salvation
for all those who obey him.

Hebrews 5:7–10 NLT

Reflect

What words, phrases, or ideas shine out to you? Why?

_____

Renew

Today I will . . .

_____

I will share what I have learned with. . .

_____

Release and Receive

Lord, today I release to You . . .

_____

I open my heart to receive from You . . .

_____

MEDITATION AND BRAIN SCIENCE

Franciscan nuns and Tibetan monks participated in scientific studies that monitored their brain activity during times of meditation and prayer. Imaging scans showed the part of the brain most lit up was the front left side, which is the region associated with clarity and happiness. Areas that were less active were the lower back part of the brain involved in fear and the fight-flight response. Both groups experienced a deep sense of well-being, peace, and joy during meditation, and this peace followed them throughout the day. Quieting the mind in meditation and prayer allowed participants to slow down automatic reactions of fear and anger and to better handle negative situations with calm.[51]

LOOK FOR THE GOOD

I will transform the Valley of Trouble into a gateway of hope.
HOSEA 2:15, NLT

There are times when unpredictable disappointment knocks us flat and we are able to quickly get up, dust off, and start again. The loss of a baby is *not* typically one of those times. It's a much slower process of plodding through the Valley of Shadows. When the stress of adjusting to loss increases, so does our tendency to track the negative. Automatic Negative Thoughts

(ANTS) gain strength and speed, making it easy to forget the good things we like about our life.

In the last journal entry, I encouraged you to list seven of your inner strengths—from creativity and perseverance to kindness and humility—and to use these assets each day for a week. Practice makes better.

This is day two of seven. Select a strength on your list and make a plan to use it each day this week. You can practice the same strength today, or work on a different one. Afterward, write about what you did, how it made you feel, and what you learned.

Consider one asset on your list from Day Six and write down how you will use it today.

Today I will use my strength by. . .

_____

Afterward, record the results.

I used my strength today by . . .

_____

Using my strength makes me feel . . .

_____

I learned . . .

_____

LIFT UP THANKS

Earlier you identified someone who has been especially kind and caring toward you in this season. I encourage you to take five minutes now to give back. Express your gratitude in a text, e-mail, or hand written note to this person.

Today I sent a note to_____ and thanked them for . . .

_____

LIGHTEN YOUR LOAD

Give God your weakness and He'll give you His strength.
ANONYMOUS

Take good care of you. Watch for signs that you are being overly hard on yourself. Dark shadows of grief can blind us to the fact that we are experiencing a temporary setback. Know that this heavy grief work doesn't last forever. If you're burdened by a sense of failure over what isn't going well and what you aren't accomplishing, it's time to STOP those ANTS (Automatic Negative Thoughts) dead in their tracks, and replace them with gentle kindness.

Today I'll STOP these ANTS . . .

- _____
- _____
- _____

I'll counter the ANTS with these kind and gentle statements . . .

- _____
- _____
- _____

BONUS VIDEO
I talk frankly about the hurtful things people say after a loss
https://youtu.be/a2QXoDPs3CM

DAY EIGHT
Responding to the Reactions of Others – Part Two

TODAY'S READING
EMPTY ARMS | CHAPTER SEVEN | PAGES 60–65

> *All told, probably more women have lost a child from this world than haven't. Most don't mention it, and they go on from day to day as if it hadn't happened, so people imagine a woman in this situation never really knew or loved what she had. But ask her sometime: how old would your child be now? And she'll know.*
>
> BARBARA KINGSOLVER

Listen To Your Heart

It's easy to let what needs to be done take priority over what needs to be lived. You don't have to move faster than you can right now. Give yourself permission to be where you are, knowing it is not where you will stay forever. How you feel is how you feel. Really, it's okay! The Valley of Shadows gives gifts, one of which is a slower pace that allows you to get to know yourself better as you listen to your heart.

Take some time now to listen to what your heart has to say.

- Using the *Feelings* list on the next page, circle the feelings you experienced while reading the second part of chapter seven in *Empty Arms*.

- Draw a double circle around one or two feelings that are most intense or that seem to stay with you longer than others. On a scale of 1-10, with 10 being most intense, identify the level of intensity by writing a number to the right of each feeling you circled.

TODAY MY HEART IS SAYING...

My Feelings

	HAPPY	SAD	ANGRY	SCARED	ASHAMED
INTENSITY OF FEELINGS	**Excited**	**Depressed**	**Furious**	**Terrified**	**Defamed**
	Overjoyed	**Agonized**	**Enraged**	**Horrified**	**Remorseful**
	Elated	**Alone**	**Outraged**	**Scared stiff**	**Dishonored**
	Thrilled	**Hurt**	**Boiling**	**Fearful**	**Admonished**
	Fired Up	**Sorrowful**	**Irate**	**Panicky**	
		Miserable	**Seething**	**Shocked**	
	Gratified	Heartbroken	Upset	Apprehensive	Apologetic
	Cheerful	Somber	Mad	Frightened	Sneaky
	Satisfied	Lost	Defended	Insecure	Guilty
	Relieved	Distressed	Frustrated	Uneasy	Secretive
	Glowing	Melancholy	Agitated	Intimidated	
		Let Down	Disgusted	Threatened	
	Glad	Unhappy	Perturbed	Nervous	Ridiculous
	Pleasant	Moody	Annoyed	Worried	Regretful
	Tender	Blue	Uptight	Timid	Pitied
	Pleased	Upset	Irritated	Unsure	Silly
	Mellow	Disappointed	Touchy	Anxious	
		Dissatisfied	Resistant	Cautious	

82

On pages 60-65 in the book I offered some ideas to consider when you're bombarded by other people's blunders as they respond to your loss. Negative ruminations over the dumb things people say drain your energy reserves. So let's do some heart work.

Using the positive perspectives below, write a personal reminder note to choose the high road of emotional freedom.

- I assume the best of others, realizing that their intentions usually are not malicious.

  Example: *Even though I'm mad about what Jennifer said, I'm going to choose to assume the best in her. I don't think she meant to be unkind.*

  Note to Self...

  _____

- I realize that careless remarks usually come from ignorance and lack of understanding.

  Example: *Brittainy has never been in my shoes, so she doesn't understand. I want her to understand, but I can be okay if she doesn't.*

  Note to Self...

  _____

- I know that the subject of death is awkward and uncomfortable for many people. Sometimes denial is the only response they know.

  Example: *Ashley may be avoiding me because she doesn't know what to say.*

  Note to Self...

  _____

- There will always be people who want to give me advice, but I always have choices. I get to decide whether or not I will use it or lose it.

- Example: *It bugs me when Emily tries to force her advice on me, but I can choose to respect her as a fellow human being, and make decisions that are best for me.*

  Note to Self…

  _____

- I refuse to hold a grudge. It's a waste of my energy and traps me in a negative spiral.

  Example: *Though a part of me wants to stay angry over what Jessica said, I choose to let it go. Rehearsing it won't help me heal.*

  Note to Self…

  _____

> *Love grows by forgiving each other constantly*
> *for not yet being who we want to be for each other.*
>
> HENRI NOUWEN

LINGER IN GOD'S LIGHT

Relax and Breathe

Inhale deeply, filling your lungs to capacity. Hold your breath for four seconds, then exhale very slowly. Notice the physical sensations of the air entering and exiting your body. Feel the relief of letting go of tension as you exhale. With each breath, invite God's love and life-giving energy to refresh you. Exhale your frustrations and stress to God. Repeat this inhale/exhale pattern four times to quiet yourself and prepare to receive from God.

Read

Invite the Holy Spirit to illumine your mind as you slowly read the following scriptures out loud. Circle words and phrases that resonate with you. Be attentive to thoughts, pictures, and impressions that surface. Don't hurry. Linger and receive.

You will **keep** in perfect **peace**
All who trust in you,
All whose thoughts are **fixed** on you!
Trust in the Lord always,
For the Lord God is the eternal Rock.

Isaiah 26:3-4 NLT

THE HEBREW MEANING OF WORDS

Keep – To watch, protect, guard as with a garrison

Fixed – To continue in a place; to take up residence, to remain, to lean upon with full reliance, rest, lay, put

Peace – *shalom* – This Hebrew word translated "peace" implies much more than mere absence of conflict. It means wholeness or well-being.

Trust – Reliance on and confidence in a person, i.e. the total trustworthiness of God, especially in relation to His promises to His people. Essentially, faith is trust in the person and character of God.[52]

Read the scripture again, this time from the Amplified Bible:

You will keep in perfect and constant peace the one whose mind is steadfast [that is, committed and focused on You—in both inclination and character], Because he trusts and takes refuge in You [with hope and confident expectation].

Trust [confidently] in the Lord forever [He is your fortress, your shield, your banner], For the Lord God is an everlasting Rock [the Rock of Ages]."

Trust God from the bottom of your heart; don't try to figure out everything on your own. Listen for God's voice in everything you do, everywhere you go; he's the one who will keep you on track. Don't assume that you know it all. Run to God! Run from evil! Your body will glow with health, your very bones will vibrate with life! Honor God with everything you own; give him the first and the best. Your barns will burst, your wine vats will brim over.

Proverbs 3:5-6 MSG

Better it is to be of a humble spirit with the meek and poor than to divide the spoil with the proud.

He who deals wisely and heeds [God's] word and counsel shall find good, and whoever leans on, trusts in, and is confident in the Lord—happy, blessed, and fortunate is he.

Proverbs 16:19-20 AMP

Reflect

What words, phrases, or ideas shine out to you? Why?

_____

_____

Renew

Today I will . . .

_____

I will share one insight with. . .

_____

Release and Receive

Lord today I release to You . . .

_____

I open my heart to receive from You . . .

_____

LOOK FOR THE GOOD

*The real voyage of discovery consists not in seeing new landscapes,
but in having new eyes.*

MARCEL PROUST

Looking for the good amplifies what is good in our lives. For the last two days, you have been using your inner assets, and intentionally sharing your strengths with others. This is day three of your seven-day focus. Select an inner quality and make a plan to use it each day this week. You can practice the same strength today, or express a different one. Afterward, write about what you did, how it made you feel, and what you learned.

Choose one asset from your list on Day Six and write down how you will use it today.

Today I will use my strength by. . .

_____

Afterward, record the results.

I used my strength today by . . .

_____

Using my strength makes me feel . . .

_____

I learned . . .

_____

_____

_____

POST-TRAUMA GROWTH AND FINDING MEANING IN LOSS

Although painful distress increases after a sudden loss, research indicates that grief can often lead to Post-Traumatic Growth if a loss challenges the mourner's assumptions and worldviews. Post-Traumatic Growth is assessed with the Post-Traumatic Growth Inventory, which measures five areas of positive change (on a 0-5 scale), in those who have experienced trauma: Relating to Others, New Possibilities, Personal Strength, Spiritual Change, and Appreciation of Life. The higher a person's ability to find meaning and make sense of their loss, the higher their Post-Traumatic Growth and the less likely they are to become entangled in Complicated Grief. A lack of meaning is associated with Complicated Grief.[53][54]

LIFT UP THANKS

And when I give thanks for the seemingly microscopic,
I make a place for God to grow within me.

ANN VOSKAMP

Giving thanks has a powerful impact on your well-being because it engages your brain in a positive cycle. Your brain only has so much power to focus its attention. It cannot easily focus on both the positive and negative at the same time. Your mind also operates with a confirmation bias. That is, it looks for things that prove what it already believes to be true. Once you start noticing the things for which you are thankful, your brain starts looking for more things that inspire you to feel grateful. The release of dopamine in your brain reinforces this, too. That's how the positive cycle works.

2-Minute Gratitude Break

In the next two minutes, quickly list as many things as you can for which you are thankful...

_____

_____

_____

_____

_____

_____

_____

THANKFULNESS AND COPING

Research from a wide array of studies shows that effective coping is one of the most salient features of grateful people. One reason that grateful people cope so effectively is because they positively reappraise negative events. The grateful processing of bad events helps bring closure and decreases the negative effect and the intrusiveness associated with troubling memories.[55]

LIGHTEN YOUR LOAD

Listen to your body. It will tell you what you need to know. You can say a polite "no" to other demands and give yourself the rest and compassion you need. Refreshing yourself makes you better able to refresh those you love. Why not take a Grief Break? Your grief will be with you for a long time, so pace yourself. Relief comes with scheduled breaks. How about jotting down some things you can do to renew? My favorite refreshers are massage, exercise, reading, and sleep. How about you?

Ways I can take a Grief Break

- _____

- _____

- _____

Today I let go of . . .

_____

_____

DAY NINE
Supporting Your Husband

TODAY'S READING
EMPTY ARMS | CHAPTER EIGHT | PAGES 67-74

A person's a person, no matter how small.

DR. SEUSS

Listen To Your Heart

This is a painful season—for your spouse as well as for you. Some days are harder than others. When we are grieving a loss we tend to stay in our heads and ruminate about the problem. We spin circles around questions like: *Why did this happen? What does it mean? What am I going to do?* Listening to your heart can stop the merry-go-round and help you settle down inside.

Listening to the language of your heart is a learned skill. It's also a slow process, much like everything else when you are grieving. There is no need to rush or strive. There is no benefit in criticizing yourself or your spouse. Loving acceptance is best. Allow each other to be wherever you are in the healing process. By attending to your emotional pain with kindness, you are less likely to wallow in self-pity. And when you are compassionate with yourself, you are better able to be compassionate with others. Mercifully approach your heartache, as you might compassionately attend to a child with a stomach ache.

When the shock of loss wears off, your awareness of all the implications suddenly increases, and so does your pain. We call this phenomenon *backdraft*, a firefighting term that describes what happens when a door in a burning house is suddenly opened. Oxygen swooshes in and flames rush out. A similar process can occur when we open the door of our hearts – love goes in and old pain comes out.[56]

Remember, you always have choices. If you find yourself flooding with overwhelming emotion, it's okay to pull back momentarily and use your calming tools to regain peace.

WHAT FATHERS EXPERIENCE AFTER PREGNANCY LOSS

Researchers interviewed fathers following pregnancy loss. Common responses were:

- frustration and helplessness due to their inability to protect their partner from emotional pain
- lack of opportunities for grieving
- lack of recognition of their anguish and grief[57]
- feeling ignored and invalidated by their support network and care providers
- survivor's guilt
- high levels of anxiety and guilt during a subsequent pregnancy and after the next child is born (experiences similar to mothers').[58]

What color are your feelings?

Color this picture in whatever colors represent your feelings today.

Take some time now to listen to what your heart has to say. I've included two Feelings lists in this chapter so you can use the second list to invite your husband or a person closely supporting you to circle the feelings that resonate with them. Identifying feelings may be new for them. You might tell them that you are learning to listen to your heart as you work through your grief. Let them know there is no wrong or right way to feel. The goal of the exercise is simply to become more aware, sensitive, and understanding of one another in your grief.

- Using the *Feelings* list on the next page, circle the feelings you experienced while reading chapter eight of *Empty Arms*.

- Draw a double circle around one or two feelings that are most intense or that seem to stay with you longer than others. On a scale of 1-10, with 10 being most intense, identify the level of intensity by writing a number to the right of each feeling you circled.

My Feelings

HAPPY	SAD	ANGRY	SCARED	ASHAMED
Excited	**Depressed**	**Furious**	**Terrified**	**Defamed**
Overjoyed	**Agonized**	**Enraged**	**Horrified**	**Remorseful**
Elated	**Alone**	**Outraged**	**Scared stiff**	**Dishonored**
Thrilled	**Hurt**	**Boiling**	**Fearful**	**Admonished**
Fired Up	**Sorrowful**	**Irate**	**Panicky**	
	Miserable	**Seething**	**Shocked**	
Gratified	Heartbroken	Upset	Apprehensive	Apologetic
Cheerful	Somber	Mad	Frightened	Sneaky
Satisfied	Lost	Defended	Insecure	Guilty
Relieved	Distressed	Frustrated	Uneasy	Secretive
Glowing	Melancholy	Agitated	Intimidated	
	Let Down	Disgusted	Threatened	
Glad	Unhappy	Perturbed	Nervous	Ridiculous
Pleasant	Moody	Annoyed	Worried	Regretful
Tender	Blue	Uptight	Timid	Pitied
Pleased	Upset	Irritated	Unsure	Silly
Mellow	Disappointed	Touchy	Anxious	
	Dissatisfied	Resistant	Cautious	

My Feelings

HAPPY	SAD	ANGRY	SCARED	ASHAMED
Excited	**Depressed**	**Furious**	**Terrified**	**Defamed**
Overjoyed	**Agonized**	**Enraged**	**Horrified**	**Remorseful**
Elated	**Alone**	**Outraged**	**Scared stiff**	**Dishonored**
Thrilled	**Hurt**	**Boiling**	**Fearful**	**Admonished**
Fired Up	**Sorrowful**	**Irate**	**Panicky**	
	Miserable	**Seething**	**Shocked**	
Gratified	Heartbroken	Upset	Apprehensive	Apologetic
Cheerful	Somber	Mad	Frightened	Sneaky
Satisfied	Lost	Defended	Insecure	Guilty
Relieved	Distressed	Frustrated	Uneasy	Secretive
Glowing	Melancholy	Agitated	Intimidated	
	Let Down	Disgusted	Threatened	
Glad	Unhappy	Perturbed	Nervous	Ridiculous
Pleasant	Moody	Annoyed	Worried	Regretful
Tender	Blue	Uptight	Timid	Pitied
Pleased	Upset	Irritated	Unsure	Silly
Mellow	Disappointed	Touchy	Anxious	
	Dissatisfied	Resistant	Cautious	

INTENSITY OF FEELINGS

Plan a convenient time to share your Feelings Chart with each other. Notice how they are similar and different. Release all expectations of having similar feelings at any given point in time. Many couples say that they notice a pattern of flip-flopping good and bad days with each other. When one feels stronger, the other feels more fragile. Everyone's grief path is unique to him or her. Accept where you are and where your spouse is today. Their grief is their grief, entirely separate from yours. Both are valid.

COUPLES WHO APPROACH VS. AVOID

Couples who engage in activities that promote approaching one another, rather than avoiding and emotional numbing after the shared trauma of having a stillborn baby, reduced Post-Traumatic Stress symptoms and increased relationship satisfaction.[59]

LINGER IN GOD'S LIGHT

Relax and Breathe

Inhale deeply, filling your lungs to capacity. Hold your breath for four seconds, then exhale very slowly. Notice the physical sensations of the air entering and exiting your body. Feel the relief of letting go of tension as you exhale. With each breath, invite God's love and life-giving energy to refresh you. Exhale your frustrations and stress to God. Repeat this inhale/exhale pattern four times to quiet yourself and prepare to receive from God.

Read

One of the most powerful ways to heal your heart is to regularly stop and enter into God's presence with an open heart. Tell Him you want the veil removed so that you can see, hear, and taste His goodness. Ask Him to shine His light into the deepest parts of your soul. Lay down the idea that you've got to figure things out or to find your way through the dark on your own. The Great Physician is with you to mend your broken heart, out in front of you orchestrating the way forward, and behind you protecting your back. Expect God to reveal whatever you need to see as you slowly read the following passages out loud. Circle words and phrases that seem to resonate with you. Be attentive to thoughts, pictures, and impressions that surface. Don't hurry. Linger and receive.

A PSALM WRITTEN BY DAVID WHEN HE WAS IN THE WILDERNESS.

O God, you are my God;
I earnestly search for you.
My soul thirsts for you;
My whole body longs for you
In this parched and weary land
Where there is no water.
I have seen you in your sanctuary
And gazed upon your power and glory.
Your unfailing love is better than life itself;
How I praise you!
I will praise you as long as I live,
Lifting up my hands to you in prayer.
You satisfy me more than the richest feast.
I will praise you with songs of joy.
I lie awake thinking of you,
Meditating on you through the night.
Because you are my helper,
I sing for joy in the shadow of your wings.
I cling to you; your strong right hand holds me securely.

Psalm 63:1-8 NLT

We know how much God loves us, and we have put our trust in his love. God is love, and all who live in love live in God, and God lives in them. And as we live in God, our love grows more perfect.

1 John 4:16-17 NLT

For in Christ, neither our most conscientious religion nor disregard of religion amounts to anything. What matters is something far more interior: faith expressed in love . . . It is absolutely clear that God has called you to a free life. Just make sure that you don't use this freedom as an excuse to do whatever you want to do and destroy your freedom. Rather, use your freedom to serve one another in love; that's how freedom grows. For everything we know about God's Word is summed up in a single sentence: Love others as you love yourself. That's an act of true freedom . . . My counsel is this: Live freely, animated and motivated by God's Spirit. Then you won't feed the compulsions of selfishness.

Galatians 5:6, 13-16 MSG

Can anything ever separate us from Christ's love? Does it mean he no longer loves us if we have trouble or calamity, or are persecuted, or hungry, or destitute, or in danger, or threatened with death? . . . No, despite all these things, overwhelming victory is ours through Christ, who loved us. And I am convinced that nothing can ever separate us from God's love. Neither death nor life, neither angels nor demons, neither our fears for today nor our worries about tomorrow—not even the powers of hell can separate us from God's love. No power in the sky above or in the earth below—indeed, nothing in all creation will ever be able to separate us from the love of God that is revealed in Christ Jesus our Lord.

Romans 8:35, 37-39 NLT

MEDITATION AND HOPE

Neuroimaging studies have documented the beneficial role of meditation in promoting the ability to regulate emotions.[60] After completing a brief guided Loving-Kindness Meditation (LKM) and Focus-Attention Meditation (FAM) training once a week for twelve weeks, participants in both groups showed decreased anxiety and negative emotion and increased hope.[61]

Reflect—

What words, phrases, or ideas shine out to you? Why?

_____

Renew

Write down one sentence from the scripture passages above that you will meditate on through the day.

_____

This is meaningful to me right now because...

_____

One insight that I will share with my husband or friend is . . .

_____

Release and Receive

Lord, today I release to You . . .

_____

I open my heart to receive from You . . .

_____

LOOK FOR THE GOOD

One of the most beautiful ways for spiritual formation to take place is to let your insecurity lead you closer to the Lord. Natural hypersensitivity can become an asset; it makes you aware of your need to be with people and it allows you to be more willing to look at their needs.

HENRI NOUWEN

Looking for the good magnifies what is good in our lives. For the past few days you have been using your inner strengths. This is day four of your seven-day focus. Select a strength and make a plan to use it in your relationship with your husband or supportive friend each day this week. You can practice the same strength today, or work on a different one. Afterward, write about what you did, how it made you feel, and what you learned.

Consider one asset from on your list from Day Six and write down how you will use it today.

_____

Today I will share my strength with my husband or friend by . . .

_____

Afterward, record the results.

I used my strength today by . . .

_____

Sharing my strength with my husband or friend made me feel . . .

_____

I learned . . .

_____

LIFT UP THANKS

2-Minute Gratitude Break - Set a timer for two minutes, then speed write until the buzzer goes off. List as many things as you can for which you are thankful...

_____

_____

_____

LIGHTEN YOUR LOAD

Learn to listen to your body. It will always tell you the truth. Pay attention to your physical reactions to people, situations, and places. You intuitively know when something feels right, wrong, or out of sync. If you carefully consider the signals it sends, your body will teach you many things about yourself, your beliefs, your life style, what to let go of, and what to embrace more fully. No matter where you are in the valley of shadows, grief breaks are necessary for recovering your balance and lightening your load.

Ways I can take a Grief Break

- By myself – 5 Minutes of Practicing the Presence of God - Place your hand on your heart while sitting quietly and 3-D breathing. Ask God to help you recall a time when you felt fully loved, accepted, believed in, protected, and safe. Sit with that memory. Pay close attention to the physical sensations attached to the memory. Soak in the feelings. Invite God to increase your capacity to sense His love and great pleasure in you. Bask in the awareness of being cherished by Him. (Feeling loved and cherished releases oxytocin in the brain which calms the body, and reassures us that everything is going to be o.k.)

- _____

- _____

- _____

Today I let go of . . .

_____

Today I will be kind to myself by . . .

_____

I will be kind to my husband by . . .

_____

_____

_____

_____

_____

_____

BONUS VIDEO
A Quick Tip For a Grief Break and Dose of Fresh Joy
https://youtu.be/7yR74vHHTCA

DAY TEN
Helping Your Children

TODAY'S READING
EMPTY ARMS | CHAPTER NINE | PAGES 75-82

> *How very softly you tiptoed into our world, almost silently, only a moment you stayed. But what an imprint your footsteps have left upon our hearts.*
>
> DOROTHY FERGUSON

Listen To Your Heart

As we are discovering more and more, feelings are an important part of who we are and how we're wired. They tell us what matters and empower us to more fully engage in love and life. Children feel the sting of loss and experience their own type of grief. It's important to help children name their pain. If they can name it, they can tame it.

Take some time now to listen to what your heart has to say. A children's *Faces Feelings Chart* follows your own *Feelings* list. If your children are two or older, plan a convenient time to meet with them and invite them to circle the faces that reflect what they feel about the baby's death.

- Using the *Feelings* list on the next page, circle the feelings you experienced while reading chapter nine of *Empty Arms*.

- Draw a double circle around one or two feelings that are most intense or that seem to stay with you longer than others. On a scale of 1-10, with 10 being most intense, identify the level of intensity by writing a number to the right of each feeling you circled.

TODAY MY HEART IS SAYING...

My Feelings

HAPPY	SAD	ANGRY	SCARED	ASHAMED
Excited	**Depressed**	**Furious**	**Terrified**	**Defamed**
Overjoyed	**Agonized**	**Enraged**	**Horrified**	**Remorseful**
Elated	**Alone**	**Outraged**	**Scared stiff**	**Dishonored**
Thrilled	**Hurt**	**Boiling**	**Fearful**	**Admonished**
Fired Up	**Sorrowful**	**Irate**	**Panicky**	
	Miserable	**Seething**	**Shocked**	
Gratified	Heartbroken	Upset	Apprehensive	Apologetic
Cheerful	Somber	Mad	Frightened	Sneaky
Satisfied	Lost	Defended	Insecure	Guilty
Relieved	Distressed	Frustrated	Uneasy	Secretive
Glowing	Melancholy	Agitated	Intimidated	
	Let Down	Disgusted	Threatened	
Glad	Unhappy	Perturbed	Nervous	Ridiculous
Pleasant	Moody	Annoyed	Worried	Regretful
Tender	Blue	Uptight	Timid	Pitied
Pleased	Upset	Irritated	Unsure	Silly
Mellow	Disappointed	Touchy	Anxious	
	Dissatisfied	Resistant	Cautious	

INTENSITY OF FEELINGS

HOW ARE YOU FEELING?

Nervous | Embarrassed | Angry | Confused | Bitter
Sad | Bored | Inferior | Content | Rejected
Loved | Numb | Furious | Friendly | Shocked
Trapped | Crazy | Hurt | Frustrated | Depressed
Lonely | Afraid | Overwhelmed | Valued | Happy
Stupid | Hopeless | Forgiven | Hopeful | Guilty

(For more excellent and colorful picture tools to raise your children's emotional intelligence, go to www.feelingsunlimited.com.)

The hardest thing today is . . .

_____

It feels risky to . . .

_____

After talking with my children about their feelings I learned . . .

_____

LINGER IN GOD'S LIGHT

Relax and Breathe

Inhale deeply, filling your lungs to capacity. Hold your breath for four seconds, then exhale very slowly. Notice the physical sensations of the air entering and exiting your body. Feel the relief of letting go of tension as you exhale. With each breath, invite God's love and life-giving energy to refresh you. Exhale your frustrations and stress to God. Repeat this inhale/exhale pattern four times to quiet yourself and prepare to receive from God.

Read

God's answer to our problems is, "Come to Me." As you get ready to spend time with God, invite the Holy Spirit to show you what you need to see. God knows all the persistent thoughts that nag at the perimeter of your peace, all those things vying for your attention. God is eager to meet with you and address the deepest needs of your heart. Slowly read the following scriptures out loud. Circle words and phrases that resonate with you. Be attentive to thoughts, pictures, and impressions that surface. Don't hurry. Linger and receive.

> Those who enter into Christ's being-here-for-us no longer have to live under a continuous, low-lying black cloud. A new power

I open my heart to receive from You . . .

LOOK FOR THE GOOD

For the last four days you have been intentionally using your inner strengths and sharing them with others as it fits into your routine. This is day five of your seven-day focus. Select a strength and make a plan to use it each day this week. You can practice the same strength each day, or work on a different one. Afterward, write about what you did, how it made you feel, and what you learned.

Select one asset on your list from Day Six and write down some ways you can use it in your relationship with your children. Write down how you will use it today. Afterward, write about what you did, how it made you feel, and what you learned.

Some ways I can use my strengths with my children are . . .

_____

Afterward, record the results.

I used my strength today by . . .

_____

When I shared my strength with my children I felt . . .

_____

I learned . . .

_____

LIFT UP THANKS

Think back to a happy memory from childhood, before you turned ten.

As I reflect on this memory the feelings and pictures that come to mind are . . .
(Use this space to write, draw, etc.)

I am thankful for . . .

- _____
- _____
- _____

LIGHTEN YOUR LOAD

Today I let go of pushing too hard and too fast by . . .

_____

Today I will be patient and kind with myself by . . .

_____

I don't have to hide my tears with my children. It is better that I don't because . . .

_____

When tears come I can . . .

_____

DAY ELEVEN
Wrestling with Your Thoughts

TODAY'S READING
EMPTY ARMS | CHAPTER TEN | PAGES 83-92

> *Some say you are too painful to remember. I say you are too precious to forget!*
>
> AUTHOR UNKNOWN

Listen To Your Heart

During this seemingly endless trek through the Valley of Shadows, you have chosen to intentionally engage and work with your grief, rather than to suppress it or allow it to run wild.

Tuning in and paying attention to the messages of your heart is a learned skill. You are intentionally shifting out of brooding over the past or worrying about the future, into being present in the *now*. Consistent practice rewires your brain.

Every moment your brain is filled with a ceaseless stream of thoughts. Scientists estimate an average of twenty-five to 125 thoughts a second. Have you ever wondered, *How many of my thoughts are telling me the truth? How many are automatic negative thoughts that began when I was child? How are my thoughts influencing my feelings?*

Thoughts are paired with an emotional charge (happy, sad, afraid, etc.). Thoughts that have intense emotional charge are known as *hot thoughts*. Hot thoughts come with hot feelings like euphoria, hopelessness, panic, or rage. Now catch this next point: It is the flow of your thoughts and feelings that determines how you experience yourself, others, life, and God. What is going on inside you, rather than outside circumstances, leads to satisfaction and meaning. The good news is, you have an incredible amount of power over which thoughts and feelings you choose to pay attention to and strengthen through the day. You can manage the information your heart gives you, so there is no need to hide from, to dismiss, or to defend against your feelings. You get to choose how you respond to your thoughts and feelings – whether to simply acknowledge them, to shift out of them into another stream of thought, or to take decisive action.

A WANDERING MIND IS AN UNHAPPY MIND

According to a Harvard research study, our minds wander about 47-48% of the time. People said they are most happy when they fully participate in the moment.[62]

Take some time now to listen to what your heart has to say.

- Using the *Feelings* list on the next page, circle the feelings you experienced while reading chapter ten of *Empty Arms*.

- Draw a double circle around one or two feelings that are most intense or that seem to stay with you longer than others. On a scale of 1-10, with 10 being most intense, identify the level of intensity by writing a number to the right of each feeling you circled.

TODAY MY HEART IS SAYING...

My Feelings

HAPPY	SAD	ANGRY	SCARED	ASHAMED
Excited	**Depressed**	**Furious**	**Terrified**	**Defamed**
Overjoyed	**Agonized**	**Enraged**	**Horrified**	**Remorseful**
Elated	**Alone**	**Outraged**	**Scared stiff**	**Dishonored**
Thrilled	**Hurt**	**Boiling**	**Fearful**	**Admonished**
Fired Up	**Sorrowful**	**Irate**	**Panicky**	
	Miserable	**Seething**	**Shocked**	
Gratified	Heartbroken	Upset	Apprehensive	Apologetic
Cheerful	Somber	Mad	Frightened	Sneaky
Satisfied	Lost	Defended	Insecure	Guilty
Relieved	Distressed	Frustrated	Uneasy	Secretive
Glowing	Melancholy	Agitated	Intimidated	
	Let Down	Disgusted	Threatened	
Glad	Unhappy	Perturbed	Nervous	Ridiculous
Pleasant	Moody	Annoyed	Worried	Regretful
Tender	Blue	Uptight	Timid	Pitied
Pleased	Upset	Irritated	Unsure	Silly
Mellow	Disappointed	Touchy	Anxious	
	Dissatisfied	Resistant	Cautious	

INTENSITY OF FEELINGS

Grief is strange. Like joy it catches us by surprise, sideways and unexpected. Part of the rhythms of this life, part of being human.

WILLIAM PAUL YOUNG

Relax and Breathe

Inhale deeply, filling your lungs to capacity. Hold your breath for four seconds, then exhale very slowly. Notice the physical sensations of the air entering and exiting your body. With each breath, invite the God Almighty, who gave you life, to fill you afresh with His Spirit. Exhale your tension. Inhale God's peace. Exhale stress. Repeat this inhale/exhale pattern four times as you prepare to receive from God.

Read

It's time to enter God's presence and let in more light. Invite the Holy Spirit to speak to your deepest longings and reveal truth that will soothe and heal. He knows well the intricacies of your heart, and the hidden needs you are unable to identify. See Jesus wrapping His peace and love around you as you slowly read the following scriptures out loud. Circle words and phrases that resonate with you. Be attentive to thoughts, pictures, and impressions that surface. Don't hurry. Linger and receive.

> Turn to me and have mercy
> For I am alone and in deep distress.
> My problems go from bad to worse.
> Oh, save me from them all!
> Feel my pain and see my trouble.
> Hear me as I pray, O Lord.
> Be merciful and answer me!
> My heart has heard you say, "Come and talk with me."

And my heart responds, "Lord I am coming."
I entrust my spirit into your hand.
Rescue me, Lord, for you are a faithful God.
I will be glad and rejoice in your unfailing love,
For you have seen my troubles,
And you care about the anguish of my soul.
Tears blur my eyes.
My body and soul are withering away.
I am dying from grief;
But I trust you, O Lord,
Saying, "You are my God!"
My future is in your hands.
So be strong and courageous,
All you who put your hope in the Lord.
The Lord says, "I will guide you along
The best pathway for your life.
I will advise you and watch over you.

Excerpts from Psalms 25, 27, 31, 32 NLT

God's eye is on those who respect him,
The ones who are looking for his love.
He's ready to come to their rescue in bad times;
In lean times he keeps body and soul together.

Psalm 33:18-19 MSG

For the word of God is living and powerful, and sharper than any two-edged sword, piercing even to the division of soul and spirit, and of joints and marrow, and is a discerner of the thoughts and intents of the heart. And there is no creature hidden from His sight, but all things are naked and open to the eyes of Him to whom we must give account.

Seeing then that we have a great High Priest who has passed through the heavens, Jesus the Son of God, let us hold fast our confession. For we do not have a High Priest who cannot sympathize with our weaknesses, but was in all points tempted as we are, yet without sin. Let us therefore come boldly to the throne of grace, that we may obtain mercy and find grace to help in time of need.

Hebrews 4:12-16 NKJV

———————

For as he thinks in his heart, so *is* he.

Proverbs 23:7 NKJV

Reflect

What words, phrases, or ideas shine out to you? Why?

_____

Renew

Today I will pay attention to . . .

_____

I will share my experience with . . .

_____

Release and Receive

Lord, today I release to You . . .

_____

_____

INTRUSIVE DOUBTS

Do you find yourself wrestling with doubts that scare you? People in thirteen countries on six continents participated in a study. 94% said they experienced unwanted thoughts and intrusive doubts.[63]

I open my heart to receive from You . . .

LOOK FOR THE GOOD

Refer back to your list of seven of your inner strengths on Day Six. You have been practicing these strengths in an effort to get out of your head and into your life. It's a healthy practice to help you keep moving forward through your grief. This is the sixth day of your seven-day focus. Select a strength from your list to express toward someone you love. Write down how you will use it today. Afterward, write about what you did, how it made you feel, and what you learned.

Today I will use one of my strengths by . . .

I expressed one of my strengths today by . . .

Using my strength makes me feel . . .

I learned . . .

LIFT UP THANKS

Our prayers for you are always spilling over into thanksgivings
COLOSSIANS 1:3

Write a prayer thanking God for the good things in your life.

_____

_____

_____

_____

_____

LIGHTEN YOUR LOAD

The cycle of endings and new beginnings is always in motion. One season ends and a new one begins. Spring always follows winter. Each season has purpose, lessons, and gifts in the eternal rhythm of our story line.

One way to lighten the heavy load of grief is to find meaning in your loss. My friend Paul says, "Either everything has meaning or nothing has meaning." Unveiling significance and perceiving the inherent value of endings and new beginnings is an ongoing process. Insights continue to emerge over time.

How does your loss speak of meaning?

• Loss opens the way for unprecedented discovery.

• _____

• _____

• _____

Who will you share an insight with today?

_____

DAY TWELVE
Enduring a Stillbirth

TODAY'S READING
EMPTY ARMS | CHAPTER ELEVEN | PAGES 93–102

> *Trust is not a once-in-a-lifetime decision, but a choice made within each moment as the river runs. We are thankful for the gifts that surround us, and then we let them go, trusting that nothing will be lost, even if we lose it for a time.*
>
> **WILLIAM PAUL YOUNG**

Listen To Your Heart

The pain and suffering of having a stillborn baby is nearly unendurable. Sufficient words escape me at the moment. A hug would be better. I am so very sorry for your loss.

The grief work you are doing is not easy, but it protects you from getting stuck in a quagmire of complicated pain. Even if you have not suffered a stillbirth, this chapter is designed to benefit you. Catastrophic loss and extreme life transitions create emotional chaos. The practices you are developing are designed to help you work with intense emotion as you move through your pain, and to usher you back into joy. As hard as it is, please trust the process. It's slow. It's challenging. But your healing will be worth it.

Take some time now to listen to what your heart has to say.

- Using the *Feelings* list on the next page, circle the feelings you experienced while reading chapter eleven of *Empty Arms*.

- Draw a double circle around one or two feelings that are most intense or that seem to stay with you longer than others. On a scale of 1-10, with 10 being most intense, identify the level of intensity by writing a number to the right of each feeling you circled.

TODAY MY HEART IS SAYING...

My Feelings

	HAPPY	SAD	ANGRY	SCARED	ASHAMED
	Excited	Depressed	Furious	Terrified	Defamed
	Overjoyed	Agonized	Enraged	Horrified	Remorseful
	Elated	Alone	Outraged	Scared stiff	Dishonored
	Thrilled	Hurt	Boiling	Fearful	Admonished
	Fired Up	Sorrowful	Irate	Panicky	
		Miserable	Seething	Shocked	
	Gratified	Heartbroken	Upset	Apprehensive	Apologetic
	Cheerful	Somber	Mad	Frightened	Sneaky
	Satisfied	Lost	Defended	Insecure	Guilty
	Relieved	Distressed	Frustrated	Uneasy	Secretive
	Glowing	Melancholy	Agitated	Intimidated	
		Let Down	Disgusted	Threatened	
	Glad	Unhappy	Perturbed	Nervous	Ridiculous
	Pleasant	Moody	Annoyed	Worried	Regretful
	Tender	Blue	Uptight	Timid	Pitied
	Pleased	Upset	Irritated	Unsure	Silly
	Mellow	Disappointed	Touchy	Anxious	
		Dissatisfied	Resistant	Cautious	

INTENSITY OF FEELINGS

The hardest thing today is . . .

My Heart Looks Like This Today . . .

Create a visual depiction of the condition of your heart. Use drawings, doodles, clip art, crayons, markers, words, quotes, and whatever helps you capture your heart in picture form.

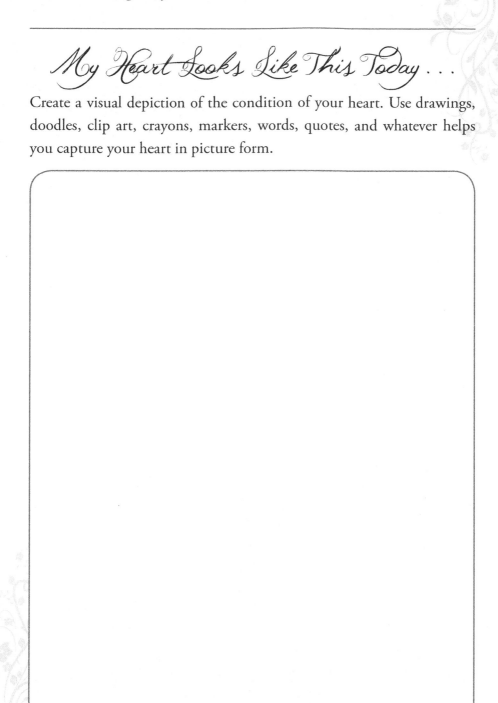

Relax and Breathe

Inhale deeply, filling your lungs to capacity. Hold your breath for four seconds, then exhale very slowly. Notice the physical sensations of the air entering and exiting your body, the air passing through your nose. Feel the relief of letting go of tension as you exhale. With each breath, invite God's healing peace to permeate your body, soul, and spirit. Exhale your troubles. Repeat this inhale/exhale pattern four times as you prepare to receive from God.

Read

Enter into the light of God's presence ready to receive whatever you need today. You can trust God to lovingly cradle your grief-torn heart. To soothe your soul in the unforced rhythms of grace. Invite the Holy Spirit to illumine the shadows as you slowly read the following scriptures out loud. Circle words and phrases that resonate with you. Be attentive to thoughts, pictures, and impressions that surface. Don't hurry. Linger and receive.

> For God, who said, "Let there be light in the darkness," has made this light shine in our hearts so we could know the glory of God that is seen in the face of Jesus Christ. We now have this light shining in our hearts, but we ourselves are like fragile clay jars containing this great treasure. This makes it clear that our great power is from God, not from ourselves.
>
> We are pressed on every side by troubles, but we are not crushed. We are perplexed, but not driven to despair. We are hunted down, but never abandoned by God. We get knocked down, but we are not destroyed. Through suffering, our bodies continue to share in the death of Jesus so that the life of Jesus may also be seen in our bodies. . .

We have the same kind of faith the Psalmist had when he said, "I believed in God, so I spoke." We know that God, who raised the Lord Jesus, will also raise us with Jesus and present us to himself together with you. All of this is for your benefit. And as God's grace reaches more and more people, there will be great thanksgiving, and God will receive more and more glory.

That is why we never give up. Though our bodies are dying, our spirits are being renewed every day. For our present troubles are small and won't last very long. Yet they produce for us a glory that vastly outweighs them and will last forever! So we don't look at the troubles we can see now; rather, we fix our gaze on things that cannot be seen. For the things we see now will soon be gone, but the things we cannot see will last forever.

For we know that when this earthly tent we live in is taken down (that is, when we die and leave this earthly body), we will have a house in heaven, an eternal body made for us by God himself and not by human hands. We grow weary in our present bodies, and we long to put on our heavenly bodies like new clothing. For we will put on heavenly bodies; we will not be spirits without bodies. While we live in these earthly bodies, we groan and sigh, but it's not that we want to die and get rid of these bodies that clothe us. Rather, we want to put on our new bodies so that these dying bodies will be swallowed up by life. God himself has prepared us for this, and as a guarantee he has given us his Holy Spirit.

So we are always confident, even though we know that as long as we live in these bodies we are not at home with the Lord. For we live by believing and not by seeing. Yes, we are fully confident, and we would rather be away from these earthly bodies, for then we will be at home with the Lord.

2 Corinthians 4:6-5:9 NLT

Jesus said, "What I am telling you is from the Father who sent me. I am telling you these things now while I am still with you. But when the Father sends the Advocate as my representative—that is, the Holy Spirit—he will teach you everything and will remind you of everything I have told you. I am leaving you with a gift—peace of mind and heart. And the peace I give is a gift the world cannot give. So don't be troubled or afraid. Remember what I told you: I am going away, but I will come back to you again. If you really loved me, you would be happy that I am going to the Father, who is greater than I am. I have told you these things before they happen so that when they do happen, you will believe."

John 14:24-29 NLT

Don't fret or worry. Instead of worrying, pray. Let petitions and praises shape your worries into prayers, letting God know your concerns. Before you know it, a sense of God's wholeness, everything coming together for good, will come and settle you down. It's wonderful what happens when Christ displaces worry at the center of your life.

Summing it all up, friends, I'd say you'll do best by filling your minds and meditating on things true, noble, reputable, authentic, compelling, gracious—the best, not the worst; the beautiful, not the ugly; things to praise, not things to curse. Do that, and God, who makes everything work together, will work you into his most excellent harmonies.

Philippians 4:6-8 MSG

Reflect

What words, phrases, or ideas shine out to you? Why?

_____

Renew

Today I will pay attention to . . .

_____

I will share my experience with . . .

_____

Release and Receive

Lord, today I release to You . . .

_____

I open my heart to receive from You . . .

_____

LOOK FOR THE GOOD

> *The greater the problem, the greater God's provision.*
> **ANONYMOUS**

Today is the seventh day of sharing your inner strengths with others. Nice work. Mindfully sharing your inner strengths with others jump starts your brain onto a positive track, when it's easily drawn to the negative. In one of your darkest seasons, you are choosing to be compassionate with yourself and mindful of others. This builds resilience and sets you up to more easily bounce back.

Select a strength from your list to express toward someone you love. Write down how you will use it today. Afterward, record what you did, how it made you feel, and what you learned.

Today I will use one of my strengths by . . .

_____

Afterward, record the results.

I expressed one of my strengths today by . . .

_____

Using my strength makes me feel . . .

_____

I learned . . .

_____

LIFT UP THANKS

Giving thanks is that: making the canyon of pain into a megaphone to proclaim the ultimate goodness of God when Satan and all the world would sneer at us to recant.

ANN VOSKAMP

What demonstrations of God's goodness are you thankful for today?

- _____

- _____

- _____

LIGHTEN YOUR LOAD

One way to lighten the heavy weight of grief is to rethink your feelings and give whatever triggered them a new meaning. When we are grieving, our minds can trick us into believing things that have no evidence or substance. After losing our baby, I created a list of faith affirmations. It's a simple way to remember what I believe, when my thoughts trigger heartache. I offer them to you to use as you wish.

Faith Affirmations

Grief screams, "God has left me. He doesn't care. I'm on my own."
Faith says, "Everything in God's economy is based on promise,
not on feelings.
God has a plan and it is good."

Despair taunts, "It's over. Forget it. You're a failure."
Faith says, "Failure is always an event, never a person. God is using
the ashes of my life to make something beautiful."

Weariness says, "You're going to be on hold forever."
Faith says, "My time is in God's hands. He will accomplish
His plans for me right on schedule."

Anguish says, "If God loved you, He would give you what you want."
Faith says, "There is a big difference between God and life.
God is always acting for my highest good."

Darkness whispers, "You can't trust God. Look at how He let you down."
Faith says, "God has proven His trustworthiness by dying for me."

Shame cries, "Your scars limit you."
Faith declares, "I am useful to God not in spite of my scars, but because of them."

Today I will remind myself . . .

_____

_____

RETHINK WHAT YOU FEEL

Neuroimaging findings show that rethinking feelings and reinterpreting the meaning of an emotional trigger reduces negative emotion to a greater extent than when we suppress and inhibit the emotion. Reappraising an emotional trigger reduces neural activation in the emotion center of the brain and enhances neural activation in the part of the brain (pre-frontal cortex) that controls emotion. Suppressing feelings demonstrated an opposite pattern.[65]

DAY THIRTEEN
Dealing with Your Postpartum Body

TODAY'S READING
EMPTY ARMS | CHAPTER TWELVE | PAGES 103-108

I held you every second of your life.
STEPHANIE PAIGE COLE

Listen To Your Heart

After a pregnancy loss you experience a wild array of confusing emotions and physical symptoms. It seems like your body has betrayed you by not giving you a healthy baby. Then, after the worst has happened, you're hit with not only deep grief, but also with the physical challenges of your body adjusting back to normal. Hormone shifts. Postpartum blues. Swelling breasts. Milk released. After-birth pain. Phantom sensations of your baby kicking inside. Fatigue. Frequent crying. Anxiety. Sleep disturbances. Headaches. Low sex drive. Fears about intercourse and a future pregnancy. With all of this going on at once, it's a wonder that you even get out of bed in the morning! And yet, courageously, you do, day after day.

You deserve to pause and take time to be kind to yourself. By tending to what is going on inside you, you honor yourself and your loss. Nothing can completely erase your pain, but daily caring for your heart is essential to your healing.

Take some time now to listen to what your heart has to say.

• Using the *Feelings* list on the next page, circle the feelings you experienced while reading chapter twelve of *Empty Arms*.

- Draw a double circle around one or two feelings that are most intense or that seem to stay with you longer than others. On a scale of 1-10, with 10 being most intense, identify the level of intensity by writing a number to the right of each feeling you circled.

My Feelings

INTENSITY OF FEELINGS	HAPPY	SAD	ANGRY	SCARED	ASHAMED
	Excited	**Depressed**	**Furious**	**Terrified**	**Defamed**
	Overjoyed	**Agonized**	**Enraged**	**Horrified**	**Remorseful**
	Elated	**Alone**	**Outraged**	**Scared stiff**	**Dishonored**
	Thrilled	**Hurt**	**Boiling**	**Fearful**	**Admonished**
	Fired Up	**Sorrowful**	**Irate**	**Panicky**	
		Miserable	**Seething**	**Shocked**	
	Gratified	Heartbroken	Upset	Apprehensive	Apologetic
	Cheerful	Somber	Mad	Frightened	Sneaky
	Satisfied	Lost	Defended	Insecure	Guilty
	Relieved	Distressed	Frustrated	Uneasy	Secretive
	Glowing	Melancholy	Agitated	Intimidated	
		Let Down	Disgusted	Threatened	
	Glad	Unhappy	Perturbed	Nervous	Ridiculous
	Pleasant	Moody	Annoyed	Worried	Regretful
	Tender	Blue	Uptight	Timid	Pitied
	Pleased	Upset	Irritated	Unsure	Silly
	Mellow	Disappointed	Touchy	Anxious	
		Dissatisfied	Resistant	Cautious	

I feel most troubled about . . .

_____

The hardest challenge with my postpartum body is . . .

_____

A good thing about slowing my pace is . . .

_____

Draw a symbolic picture of compassion holding your body.

> *The people who move in real strength and power in this world,*
> *the people whom God delights to honor, are those*
> *who are overmatched in life and know it.*
>
> RON MEHL

Relax and Breathe

Inhale deeply, filling your lungs to capacity. Hold your breath for four seconds, then exhale very slowly. Notice the physical sensations of the air entering and exiting your body. Feel the relief of letting go of tension as you exhale. With each breath, invite God's love and life-giving energy to refresh you. Exhale your frustrations and stress out to God. Repeat this inhale/exhale pattern four times to quiet yourself and prepare to receive from God.

Read

Enter into the boundless affection of God's open arms. Invite the Holy Spirit to breathe fresh wind into your spirit and chase away doubt. In the light of God's love, circle words and phrases that seem to speak loudest to you as you read. Be attentive to thoughts, pictures, and impressions that come to you. Don't hurry. Simply linger and receive.

The LORD is the everlasting God,
The Creator of all the earth.
He never grows weak or weary.
No one can measure the depths of his understanding.
He gives power to the weak
And strength to the powerless.
Even youths will become weak and tired,
And young men will fall in exhaustion.
But those who trust in the LORD will find new strength.

They will soar high on wings like eagles.
They will run and not grow weary.
They will walk and not faint.

Isaiah 40:28–31 NLT

_____

So we're not giving up. How could we!
Even though on the outside it often looks
like things are falling apart on us,
On the inside, where God is making new life,
Not a day goes by without his unfolding grace.

2 Corinthians 4:16 MSG

_____

Trust GOD from the bottom of your heart;
Don't try to figure out everything on your own.
Listen for GOD's voice in everything you do, everywhere you go;
He's the one who will keep you on track.
Don't assume that you know it all.
Run to GOD! Run from evil!
Your body will glow with health,
Your very bones will vibrate with life!

Proverbs 3:5-10 MSG

_____

Now that we know what we have—Jesus, this great High Priest with ready access to God—let's not let it slip through our fingers. We don't have a priest who is out of touch with our reality. He's been through weakness and testing, experienced it all—all but the sin. So let's walk right up to him and get what he is so ready to give. Take the mercy, accept the help.

Hebrews 4:14-16 MSG

Reflect

What words, phrases, or ideas shine out to you? Why?

_____

Renew

Today I will . . .

_____

I will share this with . . .

_____

Release and Receive

Lord, today I release to You . . .

_____

I open my heart to receive from You . . .

_____

LOOK FOR THE GOOD

Take a minute and write down three features you like best about your body.

1. _____

2. _____

3. _____

LIFT UP THANKS

Lord, today I am thankful for the good things about my body. I'm thankful that You live in me, making my body Your home. I'm thankful that my body is gradually adjusting back to normal and that this is a short-term process, *not a terminal condition. I'm thankful that You are healing me. I'm thankful that I can enjoy hot showers streaming down my back when many in this world have no running water. I'm thankful for the ability to taste wonderful flavors when many have no access to food. I'm thankful that my body can rest in safety, on a comfortable bed. I'm thankful for the smells of baking bread, fresh-cut grass, and sweet perfume. I'm thankful that I'll have a new body, free of all pain and suffering, when I get to heaven. I'm thankful that my baby never experienced the pain I've known. I'm thankful that when we meet again, we will both have glorious bodies.*

I'm thankful . . .

SEVEN BIBLE FACTS: YOUR RESURRECTED BODY IN HEAVEN

1) It will be a recognizable body (I Corinthians 15:35-49).

2) It will be a body like Christ's body (1 John 3:2).

3) It will be a body that will permit eating (Luke 24:41–43; John 21:12–13).

4) It will be a body in which the spirit predominates (1 Corinthians 15:44, 49).

5) It will be a body unlimited by time, space, or gravity (Luke 24:31; John 20:19, 26).

6) It will be an eternal body (2 Corinthians 5:1).

7) It will be a glorious body (Romans 8:18; 1 Corinthians 15:43).[66]

LIGHTEN YOUR LOAD

*One woman filled with self-love and self-acceptance
is a model more super than any cover girl.*

AMY LEIGH MERCREE

Write a compassionate note to your body regarding the many ways it serves you on a daily basis.

Dear Body of Mine,

You and I have been through a lot together. I want to take a moment to thank you for . . .

_____

_____

_____

_____

_____

_____

_____

Today I will let go of . . .

_____

_____

_____

DAY FOURTEEN
Eating for Health

TODAY'S READING
EMPTY ARMS | CHAPTER THIRTEEN | PAGES 109–118

> *A life may last just for a moment, but memory can make that moment last forever.*
>
> **AUTHOR UNKNOWN**

Listen To Your Heart

When I first came home from the hospital my appetite was gone. Planning and making meals felt like a heavy chore. I plodded through the motions, but there wasn't much pleasure in the process.

Others experience the opposite reaction. Their appetite increases and they struggle with cravings and mindless eating. It makes sense. Increased stress tends to drive increased compulsions.

The best thing we can do when we aren't where we want to be in an area of our lives is to pause, turn toward the struggle, and listen to what is going on inside our heart. It's human nature to run from pain, but healing comes when we face it and embrace it with God's help.

Take some time now to listen to what your heart has to say.

- Using the *Feelings* list on the next page, circle the feelings you experienced while reading chapter thirteen of *Empty Arms*.

- Draw a double circle around one or two feelings that are most intense or that seem to stay with you longer than others. On a scale of 1-10, with 10 being most intense, identify the level of intensity by writing a number to the right of each feeling you circled.

TODAY MY HEART IS SAYING...

My Feelings

HAPPY	SAD	ANGRY	SCARED	ASHAMED
Excited	**Depressed**	**Furious**	**Terrified**	**Defamed**
Overjoyed	**Agonized**	**Enraged**	**Horrified**	**Remorseful**
Elated	**Alone**	**Outraged**	**Scared stiff**	**Dishonored**
Thrilled	**Hurt**	**Boiling**	**Fearful**	**Admonished**
Fired Up	**Sorrowful**	**Irate**	**Panicky**	
	Miserable	**Seething**	**Shocked**	
Gratified	Heartbroken	Upset	Apprehensive	Apologetic
Cheerful	Somber	Mad	Frightened	Sneaky
Satisfied	Lost	Defended	Insecure	Guilty
Relieved	Distressed	Frustrated	Uneasy	Secretive
Glowing	Melancholy	Agitated	Intimidated	
	Let Down	Disgusted	Threatened	
Glad	Unhappy	Perturbed	Nervous	Ridiculous
Pleasant	Moody	Annoyed	Worried	Regretful
Tender	Blue	Uptight	Timid	Pitied
Pleased	Upset	Irritated	Unsure	Silly
Mellow	Disappointed	Touchy	Anxious	
	Dissatisfied	Resistant	Cautious	

INTENSITY OF FEELINGS

THE POWER OF MINDFUL EATING

Surveys show that 50 to 60 percent of women eat for emotional reasons rather than because of hunger. The stress of difficult emotions dampens the reward response in the brain and causes craving, which is what drives overeating. Researchers have considered the role of stress on overeating. The study showed that the more the women practiced living in the present and paying attention to their inner voice, the greater decrease they saw in their anxiety, chronic stress, and deep belly fat. Women in the mindfulness program maintained their body weight while the women in the control group increased their weight over the same period of time. Mastering simple mindful eating and stress-reduction techniques helped prevent weight gain even without dieting.[67]

It's easiest for me to eat healthy when . . .

_____

I can simply modify my food choices by . . .

_____

If I adjust my food choices just for today, I'd likely feel . . .

_____

Things that get in my way of eating for health are . . .

_____

I can face the things that have been getting in my way and make an adjustment by . . .

_____

My vulnerable times for mindlessly eating are . . . (usually when we are multitasking and not paying attention)

_____

I can give, become more aware, and plan around those vulnerable times by . . .

_____

I can comfort myself in ways other than with food by . . .

_____

I can celebrate and reward myself when I eat for health by . . .

_____

When compulsive cravings come, I can try these five steps:

1. Give myself the gift of a time-out and pay attention to what is going on inside me.

2. Ask God for wisdom: "What is driving this compulsion? Is there something I'm not facing?"

3. Compassionately explore and name the emotions underneath the physical cravings. (Am I feeling irritated, frustrated, annoyed, anxious, sad, bored, stressed, rushed, or hungry? See your *Feelings* list.) What triggered the cravings?

4. Distinguish between what I want and what I need, and then make a conscious choice.

5. Be thankful that I tuned in and interrupted a mindless automatic reaction that can diminish my well-being.

BARRIERS TO WEIGHT LOSS

Two barriers to long-term weight loss are 1) reward-driven eating (lack of control over eating, preoccupations with food, lack of satiety) and 2) psychological stress. Researchers compared the effects of a five-and-a-half-month diet and exercise intervention with or without mindfulness training on weight loss among adults with obesity. The group using mindfulness tools had significant reductions in reward-driven eating at six month post-intervention, which, in turn, predicted weight loss at twelve months.[68]

LINGER IN GOD'S LIGHT

Relax and Breathe

Inhale deeply, filling your lungs to capacity. Hold your breath for four seconds, then exhale very slowly. Notice the physical sensations of the air entering and exiting your body. Feel the relief of letting go of tension as you exhale. With each breath, invite the God Almighty, who gave you life, to fill you afresh with His Spirit. Exhale stress out. Repeat this inhale/exhale pattern four times to quiet yourself and prepare to receive from God.

Read

Invite the Holy Spirit to illumine your mind as you slowly read the following scriptures out loud. Circle words and phrases that resonate with you. Be attentive to thoughts, pictures, and impressions that surface. Don't hurry. Linger and receive.

Jesus said, "Don't waste your energy striving for perishable food like that. Work for the food that sticks with you, food that nourishes your lasting life, food the Son of Man provides. He and what he does are guaranteed by God the Father to last."

To that they said, "Well, what do we do then to get in on God's works?"

Jesus said, "Throw your lot in with the One that God has sent. That kind of a commitment gets you in on God's works."

They waffled: "Why don't you give us a clue about who you are, just a hint of what's going on? When we see what's up, we'll commit ourselves. Show us what you can do. Moses fed our ancestors with bread in the desert. It says so in the Scriptures: 'He gave them bread from heaven to eat.' "

Jesus responded, "The real significance of that Scripture is not that Moses gave you bread from heaven but that my Father is right now offering you bread from heaven, the real bread. The Bread of God came down out of heaven and is giving life to the world."

They jumped at that: "Master, give us this bread, now and forever!"

Jesus said, "I am the Bread of Life. The person who aligns with me hungers no more and thirsts no more, ever. I have told you this explicitly because even though you have seen me in action, you don't really believe me. Every person the Father gives me eventually comes running to me. And once that person is with me, I hold on and don't let go. I came down from heaven not to follow my own whim but to accomplish the will of the One who sent me.

"This, in a nutshell, is that will: that everything handed over to me by the Father be completed—not a single detail missed— and at the wrap-up of time I have everything and everyone put together, upright and whole. This is what my Father wants: that anyone who sees the Son and trusts who he is and what he does and then aligns with him will enter real life, eternal life. My part is to put them on their feet alive and whole at the completion of time. . . The Father who sent me is in charge. He draws people to me—that's the only way you'll ever come. This is what the prophets meant when they wrote, 'And then they will all be personally taught by God.' Anyone who has spent any time at all listening to the Father, really listening and therefore learning, comes to me to be taught personally—to see it with his own eyes, hear it with his own ears, from me, since I have it firsthand from the Father. No one has seen the Father except the One who has his Being alongside the Father—and you can see me.

"I am telling you the most solemn and sober truth now: Whoever believes in me has real life, eternal life. I am the Bread of Life. Anyone eating this Bread will not die, ever. I am the Bread—living bread! —who came down out of heaven. Anyone who eats this Bread will live—and forever!"

John 6:27-51 MSG

On the final and climactic day of the Feast, Jesus took his stand. He cried out, "If anyone thirsts, let him come to me and drink. Rivers of living water will brim and spill out of the depths of anyone who believes in me this way, just as the Scripture says." (He said this in regard to the Spirit, whom those who believed in him were about to receive.)

John 7:37-39 MSG

Reflect

What shines out to you? Why?

_____

Renew

Today I will take one step toward eating for health . . .

_____

I will share this plan with . . .

_____

Release and Receive

Lord, today I release to You . . .

_____

I open my heart to receive from You . . .

_____

LOOK FOR THE GOOD

> *"Open your mouth and taste, open your eyes and see how good GOD is. Blessed are you who run to Him. Worship GOD if you want the best; Worship opens doors to all his goodness."*
>
> PSALM 34:8-9 MSG

Record three ways that God has displayed His goodness to you.

1. _____

2. _____

3. _____

LIFT UP THANKS

I'm thankful . . .

_____

I'm thankful . . .

_____

I'm thankful . . .

_____

LIGHTEN YOUR LOAD

I encourage you to let go of the "shoulds" and "should nots" around food. Instead, shift your attention to discovering what and how you can eat in ways that make you feel healthy and well.

Today I let go of . . .

_____

_____

_____

_____

_____

_____

DAY FIFTEEN
Boosting Your Mood with Exercise

TODAY'S READING
EMPTY ARMS | CHAPTER FOURTEEN | PAGES 119–124

> *Sometimes the smallest things take up the most room in your heart.*
>
> A.A. MILNE

Listen To Your Heart

Grief is a force that sends you spinning toward the edges of crazy. It's as if you've been thrown into turbulent whitewater and the water is taking you wherever it wants. There are moments when riptides suck you under and you're certain you'll never come up again. But you do. It's calm for a bit, and then, *whoosh*, you're slammed up against a rock. More calm. More waves. But, eventually, the river carries you into a wide-open body of water and leaves you in a better place. Fighting and ignoring the process doesn't help. Going with the flow as best you can and listening to your heart does.

Take some time now to listen to what your heart has to say.

- Using the *Feelings* list on the next page, circle the feelings you experienced while reading chapter fourteen of *Empty Arms*.

- Draw a double circle around one or two feelings that are most intense or that seem to stay with you longer than others. On a scale of 1-10, with 10 being most intense, identify the level of intensity by writing a number to the right of each feeling you circled.

TODAY MY HEART IS SAYING...

My Feelings

	HAPPY	SAD	ANGRY	SCARED	ASHAMED
	Excited	**Depressed**	**Furious**	**Terrified**	**Defamed**
	Overjoyed	**Agonized**	**Enraged**	**Horrified**	**Remorseful**
	Elated	**Alone**	**Outraged**	**Scared stiff**	**Dishonored**
	Thrilled	**Hurt**	**Boiling**	**Fearful**	**Admonished**
	Fired Up	**Sorrowful**	**Irate**	**Panicky**	
		Miserable	**Seething**	**Shocked**	
	Gratified	Heartbroken	Upset	Apprehensive	Apologetic
	Cheerful	Somber	Mad	Frightened	Sneaky
	Satisfied	Lost	Defended	Insecure	Guilty
	Relieved	Distressed	Frustrated	Uneasy	Secretive
	Glowing	Melancholy	Agitated	Intimidated	
		Let Down	Disgusted	Threatened	
	Glad	Unhappy	Perturbed	Nervous	Ridiculous
	Pleasant	Moody	Annoyed	Worried	Regretful
	Tender	Blue	Uptight	Timid	Pitied
	Pleased	Upset	Irritated	Unsure	Silly
	Mellow	Disappointed	Touchy	Anxious	
		Dissatisfied	Resistant	Cautious	

INTENSITY OF FEELINGS

EXERCISE CHANGES THE BRAIN

Research shows that physical exercise changes the structure and function of the brain. Studies in animals and people have shown that physical activity generally increases brain volume and can reduce the number and size of age-related holes in the brain's white and gray matter. It promotes the creation of new brain cells and increases the number of cells in the hippocampus. Depression also correlates with fewer cells in the hippocampus.[69]

It's easiest for me to exercise when . . .

_____

I can simply adjust my activity level by . . .

_____

If I modify my activity level just for this week I might feel. . .

_____

Things that get in my way of exercise right now are . . .

_____

I can manage the things that have been getting in my way and make adjustments by . . .

_____

My vulnerable times for talking myself out of exercise are . . .

_____

I can become more aware and plan around these vulnerable times by . . .

_____

I can celebrate and reward myself when I am more physically active by . . .

If I start talking myself out of exercising I can try these five steps:

1. I can give myself the gift of a time-out and pay attention to what is going on inside me.

2. Ask God for wisdom: "What is driving this avoidance?"

3. I can compassionately explore and name the emotions underneath the avoidance, without judgment or criticism. Am I feeling sad, tired, hopeless, annoyed, hurt, ashamed, lazy, or other? (See your *Feelings* list.)

4. I can distinguish between what I want and what I need, and then make a conscious choice.

5. I can be thankful that I tuned in, interrupted the avoidance, and grew in emotional awareness.

EXERCISE CALMS AND HELPS DEPRESSED MOOD

University researchers revealed that exercising stimulates the production of new neurons, including those that release the neurotransmitter GABA. GABA inhibits excessive neuronal firing, helping to induce a natural state of calm. Depression is often characterized by depleted glutamate and GABA, which return to normal when mental health is restored. Exercise activates the metabolic pathway that replenishes these neurotransmitters.[70]

LINGER IN GOD'S LIGHT

Relax and Breathe

Inhale deeply, filling your lungs to capacity. Hold your breath for four seconds, then exhale very slowly. Notice the physical sensations of the air entering and exiting your body. Feel the relief of letting go of tension as you exhale. With each breath, invite God to fill you afresh with His Spirit. Exhale stress out. Repeat this inhale/exhale pattern four times to quiet yourself and prepare to receive from God.

Read

Invite the Holy Spirit to illumine your mind as you slowly read the following scriptures out loud. Circle words and phrases that resonate with you. Be attentive to thoughts, pictures, and impressions that surface. Don't hurry. Linger and receive.

> GOD, investigate my life;
> Get all the facts firsthand.
> I'm an open book to you;
> Even from a distance, you know what I'm thinking.
> You know when I leave and when I get back;
> I'm never out of your sight.
> You know everything I'm going to say
> Before I start the first sentence.
> I look behind me and you're there,
> Then up ahead and you're there, too—
> Your reassuring presence, coming and going.
> This is too much, too wonderful—
> I can't take it all in! . . .
> Is there any place I can go to avoid your Spirit?
> To be out of your sight?
> If I climb to the sky, you're there!

If I go underground, you're there!
If I flew on morning's wings
To the far western horizon,
You'd find me in a minute—
You're already there waiting!
Then I said to myself, "Oh, he even sees me in the dark!
At night I'm immersed in the light!"
It's a fact: darkness isn't dark to you;
Night and day, darkness and light, they're all the same to you.

Psalm 139:1-12 MSG

———————

Blessed be the name of God,
Forever and ever.
He knows all, does all:
He changes the seasons and guides history,
He raises up kings and also brings them down,
He provides both intelligence and discernment,
He opens up the depths, tells secrets,
Sees in the dark—light spills out of him!
God of all my ancestors, all thanks! all praise!
You made me wise and strong.
And now you've shown us what we asked for.

Daniel 2:20-23 MSG

———————

He uncovers mysteries hidden in darkness;
He brings light to the deepest gloom.

Job 12:22 NLT

Workouts in the gymnasium are useful, but a disciplined life in God is far more so, making you fit both today and forever. You can count on this. Take it to heart.

I Timothy 4:8-9 MSG

Reflect

What words, phrases, or ideas shine out to you? Why?

_____

Renew

Today I will remember . . .

_____

I will share this with . . .

_____

Release and Receive

Lord, today I release to You . . .

_____

I open my heart to receive from You . . .

_____

LOOK FOR THE GOOD

Write down three good things you can add to your day.

1. _____

2. _____

3. _____

GRATITUDE AND EXERCISE

Researchers compared three groups of people who journaled daily. The gratitude group that recorded what they were thankful for showed significant differences from the others. They were 25 percent happier, more optimistic about the future, felt better about their lives, and even exercised nearly one and a half hours more a week than those who journaled about their weekly events or hassles.[71]

LIFT UP THANKS

Who are you thankful for in your life today? Why?

I'm thankful for _____ *because* _____

I'm thankful for _____ *because* _____

I'm thankful for _____ *because* _____

How about sending one or more of them a message to let them know?

_____

LIGHTEN YOUR LOAD

Focusing on all the "shoulds" and "should nots" around exercise will sap your energy and motivation. Instead, shift your attention to planning one simple step you can take to add more activity into your life to improve your well-being.

Today I let go of . . .

_____

_____

DAY SIXTEEN
Surviving The Trauma Of A Tubal Pregnancy

TODAY'S READING

EMPTY ARMS | CHAPTER FIFTEEN | PAGES 125-136

> *Losses do that. One life-loss can infect the whole of a life. Like a rash that wears through our days, our sight becomes peppered with black voids. Now everywhere we look, we only see all that isn't: holes, lack, deficiency.*
>
> ANN VOSKAMP

Listen To Your Heart

Even if you have not suffered a tubal pregnancy, this chapter is designed to benefit you. Following any pregnancy loss, grief tends to feel like a dark funnel sucking us into a bottomless abyss. A downward spiral of fear, anger, and sickening sadness lures us to draw dark conclusions. *I'm miserable. I'm abandoned. Things are never going to work out. I'm a failure. Everybody else gets the 'good'.*

We can deny, hide, and pretend that the feelings don't exist, or we can pause, acknowledge, and let the feelings go. Living in the light and being emotionally honest is the path of healing. The truth sets you free.

Take some time now to listen to what your heart has to say.

- Using the *Feelings* list on the next page, circle the feelings you experienced while reading chapter fifteen of *Empty Arms*.

- Draw a double circle around one or two feelings that are most intense or that seem to stay with you longer than others. On a scale of 1-10, with 10 being most intense, identify the level of intensity by writing a number to the right of each feeling you circled.

My Feelings

HAPPY	SAD	ANGRY	SCARED	ASHAMED
Excited	**Depressed**	**Furious**	**Terrified**	**Defamed**
Overjoyed	**Agonized**	**Enraged**	**Horrified**	**Remorseful**
Elated	**Alone**	**Outraged**	**Scared stiff**	**Dishonored**
Thrilled	**Hurt**	**Boiling**	**Fearful**	**Admonished**
Fired Up	**Sorrowful**	**Irate**	**Panicky**	
	Miserable	**Seething**	**Shocked**	
Gratified	Heartbroken	Upset	Apprehensive	Apologetic
Cheerful	Somber	Mad	Frightened	Sneaky
Satisfied	Lost	Defended	Insecure	Guilty
Relieved	Distressed	Frustrated	Uneasy	Secretive
Glowing	Melancholy	Agitated	Intimidated	
	Let Down	Disgusted	Threatened	
Glad	Unhappy	Perturbed	Nervous	Ridiculous
Pleasant	Moody	Annoyed	Worried	Regretful
Tender	Blue	Uptight	Timid	Pitied
Pleased	Upset	Irritated	Unsure	Silly
Mellow	Disappointed	Touchy	Anxious	
	Dissatisfied	Resistant	Cautious	

INTENSITY OF FEELINGS

I feel most confused about . . .

_____

The hardest challenge for me right now is . . .

_____

Draw a symbolic picture of love cradling your baby.

LINGER IN GOD'S LIGHT

The edges of God are tragedy. The depths of God are joy, beauty, resurrection, life. Resurrection answers crucifixion; life answers death.

MARJORIE HEWITT SUCHOCK

Relax and Breathe

Inhale deeply, filling your lungs to capacity. Hold your breath for four seconds, then exhale very slowly. Notice the physical sensations of the air entering and exiting your body. Feel the relief of letting go of tension as you exhale. With each breath, invite God to fill you afresh with His Spirit. Exhale stress out. Repeat this inhale/exhale pattern four times to quiet yourself and prepare to receive from God.

Read

Invite the Holy Spirit to illumine your mind as you slowly read the following scriptures out loud. Circle words and phrases that resonate with you. Be attentive to thoughts, pictures, and impressions that surface. Don't hurry. Linger and receive.

> In the crowd that day there was a woman who for twelve years had been afflicted with hemorrhages. She had spent every penny she had on doctors but not one had been able to help her. She slipped in from behind and touched the edge of Jesus' robe. At that very moment her hemorrhaging stopped. Jesus said, "Who touched me?"

> When no one stepped forward, Peter said, "But Master, we've got crowds of people on our hands. Dozens have touched you."

Jesus insisted, "Someone touched me. I felt power discharging from me."

When the woman realized that she couldn't remain hidden, she knelt trembling before him. In front of all the people, she blurted out her story—why she touched him and how at that same moment she was healed.

Jesus said, "Daughter, you took a risk trusting me, and now you're healed and whole. Live well, live blessed!"

Luke 8:43-48 MSG

Jesus said, "God's Spirit is on me; He's chosen me to preach the Message of good news to the poor, Sent me to announce pardon to prisoners and Recovery of sight to the blind, To set the burdened and battered free, to announce, 'This is God's year to act!'"

Luke 4:18-19 MSG

They said, "Put your entire trust in the Master Jesus. Then you'll live as you were meant to live—and everyone in your house included!"

Acts 16:30 MSG

Reflect

What shines out to you? Why?

_____

Renew

Today I will . . .

_____

I will share this with . . .

_____

Release and Receive

Lord, today I release to You . . .

_____

I open my heart to receive from You. . .

_____

LOOK FOR THE GOOD

Grief distorts your perception, making it hard to see the good that is always around you. You can clear the fog by *planning good* into your schedule, and making it happen. Rather than pushing yourself to get more things done, try weaving three enjoyable pleasures into your day. You might consider:

- something you do alone (reading, music, pedicure)

- something you do with another (play a game, watch a movie, meet for coffee)

- something meaningful (an activity that renews your body, soul, spirit; assist another in need through a random act of kindness.

THE POWER OF PLANNING GOOD INTO YOUR DAY

A study found that 52 moderately to severely depressed people, hospitalized with suicidal thoughts, found planning something good into their day easy and valuable. They reported less hopelessness and more optimism after participating in the exercise.[72]

Today I will plan three good things into my day:

1. _____

2. _____

3. _____

> *Practice is the hardest part of learning,*
> *and training is the essence of transformation.*
>
> ANN VOSKAMP

LIFT UP THANKS

I'm thankful . . .

_____

I'm thankful . . .

_____

I'm thankful . . .

_____

LIGHTEN YOUR LOAD

Write a compassionate thank you note to yourself for persevering day after day through the hard work of grief. You are taking time to care for your broken heart and let go of the pain.

- Mention some of the meaningful insights you have gleaned along the way.

- Note what you want to let go of a little more today.

- Be specific about what you want to set aside and "let be."

Dear Me,

I want to take a moment to thank you for persisting in the midst of such great sadness. This road through the Valley of Shadows is not easy . . .

_____

_____

_____

_____

_____

_____

_____

_____

_____

_____

_____

_____

_____

_____

_____

_____

_____

_____

_____

_____

_____

_____

_____

_____

DAY SEVENTEEN
Beginning Again

TODAY'S READING
EMPTY ARMS | CHAPTER SIXTEEN | PAGES 137-144

> *Where we find difficulty we may always expect*
> *that a discovery awaits us.*
>
> C. S. LEWIS

Listen To Your Heart

Day by day, hour by hour, you are moving forward *through* your grief. You are choosing to linger in the light and to look for eternal riches. You're fanning the flames of gratitude by thanking God for who you are, including all your strengths and vulnerabilities, and for what you came here to do, even if the purpose doesn't seem clear. You are honoring God by living in the wide-open spaces of His grace, paying attention to your heart, dealing with your feelings, trusting Him to transform, and practicing habits that heal.

Take some time now to listen to what your heart has to say.

- Using the *Feelings* list on the next page, circle the feelings you experienced while reading chapter sixteen of *Empty Arms*.

- Draw a double circle around one or two feelings that are most intense or that seem to stay with you longer than others. On a scale of 1-10, with 10 being most intense, identify the level of intensity by writing a number to the right of each feeling you circled.

TODAY MY HEART IS SAYING...

My Feelings

HAPPY	SAD	ANGRY	SCARED	ASHAMED
Excited	**Depressed**	**Furious**	**Terrified**	**Defamed**
Overjoyed	**Agonized**	**Enraged**	**Horrified**	**Remorseful**
Elated	**Alone**	**Outraged**	**Scared stiff**	**Dishonored**
Thrilled	**Hurt**	**Boiling**	**Fearful**	**Admonished**
Fired Up	**Sorrowful**	**Irate**	**Panicky**	
	Miserable	**Seething**	**Shocked**	
Gratified	Heartbroken	Upset	Apprehensive	Apologetic
Cheerful	Somber	Mad	Frightened	Sneaky
Satisfied	Lost	Defended	Insecure	Guilty
Relieved	Distressed	Frustrated	Uneasy	Secretive
Glowing	Melancholy	Agitated	Intimidated	
	Let Down	Disgusted	Threatened	
Glad	Unhappy	Perturbed	Nervous	Ridiculous
Pleasant	Moody	Annoyed	Worried	Regretful
Tender	Blue	Uptight	Timid	Pitied
Pleased	Upset	Irritated	Unsure	Silly
Mellow	Disappointed	Touchy	Anxious	
	Dissatisfied	Resistant	Cautious	

INTENSITY OF FEELINGS

Looking forward I feel . . .

_____

I wonder . . .

_____

I long to . . .

_____

I can see myself down the road . . .

_____

_____*makes me smile.*

LINGER IN GOD'S LIGHT

Let it be your business to keep your mind in the presence of the Lord. If it sometimes wanders and withdraws itself from Him, do not disquiet yourself for that: Trouble and disquiet serve to distract the mind rather than to re-collect it: The will must bring it back into tranquility.

BROTHER LAWRENCE

Relax and Breathe

Inhale deeply, filling your lungs to capacity. Hold your breath for four seconds, then exhale very slowly. Notice the physical sensations of the air entering and exiting your body. Feel the relief of letting go of tension as you exhale. With each breath, invite God to fill you afresh with His Spirit. Exhale stress out. Repeat this inhale/exhale pattern four times to quiet yourself and prepare to receive from God.

Read

Invite the Holy Spirit to illumine your mind as you slowly read the following scriptures out loud. Circle words and phrases that resonate with you. Be attentive to thoughts, pictures, and impressions that surface. Don't hurry. Linger and receive.

I cry out to God; yes, I shout.
Oh, that God would listen to me!
When I was in deep trouble,
I searched for the Lord.
All night long I prayed, with hands lifted toward heaven,
But my soul was not comforted.
I think of God, and I moan,
Overwhelmed with longing for his help.
You don't let me sleep.
I am too distressed even to pray!
I think of the good old days,
Long since ended,
When my nights were filled with joyful songs.
I search my soul and ponder the difference now.
Has the Lord rejected me forever?
Will he never again be kind to me?
Is his unfailing love gone forever?
Have his promises permanently failed?
Has God forgotten to be gracious?
Has he slammed the door on his compassion?
And I said, "This is my fate;
The Most High has turned his hand against me."
But then I *recall* all you have done, O LORD;
I remember your wonderful deeds of long ago.
They are constantly in my thoughts.
I cannot stop thinking about your mighty works

O God, your ways are holy.
Is there any god as mighty as you?
You are the God of great wonders!

Psalm 77:1-14 NLT

I lie awake thinking of you,
Meditating on you through the night.
Because you are my helper,
I sing for joy in the shadow of your wings.
I cling to you;
Your strong right hand holds me securely.

Psalm 63:6-8 NLT

Think back on those early days when you were first enlightened.
Remember how you remained faithful even though it meant
terrible suffering.
Sometimes you were exposed to public ridicule and were beaten,
And sometimes you helped others who were suffering the
same things.
You suffered along with those who were thrown into jail,
And when all you owned was taken from you, you accepted it
with joy.
You knew there were better things waiting for you that will
last forever.
So do not throw away this confident trust in the Lord.
Remember the great reward it brings you!

Hebrews 10:32-36 NLT

RECALL = HOPE

The English word *recall* in Psalm 77:11 is translated from the Hebrew verb *hagah*, which means "to muse, meditate, to be mindful of, moan, think, or speak." In times of distress, trouble, or oppression, David would *hagah* the Lord (Psalms 63:6; 77:12; 143:5). The word refers to inner mindfulness and outward expressions. God Himself uses *hagah* when he tells Joshua to encourage all the people to meditate on Scripture day and night. This was key to their personal happiness and success (Joshua 1:8).[73]

Reflect

What shines out to you? Why?

_____

_____

Renew

Today I will . . . .

_____

_____

I will share this with . . .

_____

_____

Release and Receive

Lord, today I release to You . . .

_____

_____

I open my heart to receive from You . . .

_____

_____

LOOK FOR THE GOOD

Grief can cause us to forget. We forget that loss does not stop God from continuing the good work He began in us. We forget that delays don't necessarily mean denials. We forget that God is for us, not against us. We forget that we are not forgotten.

David was having one of those forgetful moments in Psalm 77, until he started writing verse 11. Then, suddenly, everything shifted. What happened? David *recalled*. He became mindful of the good things God had already done, and this gave a whole different perspective.

Do you want a simple way to disarm discouragement? Remember the good things God has already done in your life. Let's do that now. Jot down some of the ways you have experienced the goodness of God in the distant or recent past.

- _____
- _____
- _____

LIFT UP THANKS

> *And I will give you treasures hidden in the darkness — secret riches. I will do this so you may know that I am the LORD, the God of Israel, the one who calls you by name.*
>
> ISAIAH 45:3 NLT

You have gained insight and wisdom in the Valley of Shadows. There are many positive ways you have grown. You're not the same person you were before you began this season of mourning and intentional healing. How about lifting up thanks for a few of the specific treasures you've found hidden in the darkness?

I'm thankful . . .

_____

I'm thankful . . .

_____

I'm thankful . . .

_____

LIGHTEN YOUR LOAD

No one can fully know the pain you've experienced since losing your baby. Your suffering is unique to you because you and your circumstances are unique. That is why the journey through grief feels like such a solitary experience. However, though grief is lonely, we dare not try to trek through the shadows without companions. We may enter the Valley of Shadows alone, but once there, we must open our hearts and let others compassionately hold the pain with us. No, you don't have the energy to invite everyone into your inner circle. The goal of connecting with others during grief is to lighten your load, not add to it. Making a discerning choice to open up with one or two safe friends can provide security and comfort when it feels like your world has fallen apart.

WELL-BEING AND RELATIONSHIPS

An analysis of 148 research studies with more than 308,000 participants looked at how relationships impact health and mortality. The results showed that not having meaningful connections with family and friends can be as bad for a person's well-being as well-established risk factors such as smoking, alcoholism, physical inactivity, and obesity.[75]

You can keep this simple: take a coffee break with a friend at work, share an experience with a relative over the phone, go for a walk with a confidante, or visit a church. Cultivate relationships with those who matter to you. Joy and healing come in the context of relationships. Don't wait for someone else to make the first move. People are often tentative about initiating with those who are mourning. They feel uneasy about what to say, and are hesitant to intrude on your privacy.

- Whom do you know who has a way of making you feel safe and good about yourself? (They tend to be compassionate, listen well, are comfortable in their own skin, and genuinely accept others.)

- What have they done or said that was meaningful to you after they learned about the loss of your baby?

- What is one small way you can nurture this relationship today?

BONUS VIDEO
Use Your Voice
https://youtu.be/V4XFfio9GeQ

GIRLFRIENDS MATTER!

Researchers concluded after a twenty-year study with more than 4,700 participants that a person's happiness depends on the happiness of others with whom they are connected. Happiness is contagious, and it spreads significantly through relationships with the same gender rather than with the opposite sex. People who are surrounded by many happy people are more likely to be happy in the future.[74]

DAY EIGHTEEN
Celebrating Your Baby

TODAY'S READING
EMPTY ARMS | CHAPTER SEVENTEEN | PAGES 145-150

> *There is no foot so small that it cannot leave an imprint on this world.*
>
> **AUTHOR UNKNOWN**

Listen To Your Heart

We learn something valuable, if we're open to it, from all of our experiences. Traveling through the Valley of Shadows teaches, transforms, and provides a place for discovering truth. You have chosen the high road of healing. You refuse to see, think, and feel from a victim's point of view. Rather than standing on the edge of life cowering and closed, you courageously turn towards your heart, engage with your grief, and give it a voice.

Take some time now to listen to what your heart has to say.

- Using the *Feelings* list on the next page, circle the feelings you experienced while reading chapter seventeen of *Empty Arms*.

- Draw a double circle around one or two feelings that are most intense or that seem to stay with you longer than others. On a scale of 1-10, with 10 being most intense, identify the level of intensity by writing a number to the right of each feeling you circled.

TODAY MY HEART IS SAYING...

My Feelings

	HAPPY	SAD	ANGRY	SCARED	ASHAMED
	Excited	**Depressed**	**Furious**	**Terrified**	**Defamed**
	Overjoyed	**Agonized**	**Enraged**	**Horrified**	**Remorseful**
	Elated	**Alone**	**Outraged**	**Scared stiff**	**Dishonored**
	Thrilled	**Hurt**	**Boiling**	**Fearful**	**Admonished**
	Fired Up	**Sorrowful**	**Irate**	**Panicky**	
		Miserable	**Seething**	**Shocked**	
	Gratified	Heartbroken	Upset	Apprehensive	Apologetic
	Cheerful	Somber	Mad	Frightened	Sneaky
	Satisfied	Lost	Defended	Insecure	Guilty
	Relieved	Distressed	Frustrated	Uneasy	Secretive
	Glowing	Melancholy	Agitated	Intimidated	
		Let Down	Disgusted	Threatened	
	Glad	Unhappy	Perturbed	Nervous	Ridiculous
	Pleasant	Moody	Annoyed	Worried	Regretful
	Tender	Blue	Uptight	Timid	Pitied
	Pleased	Upset	Irritated	Unsure	Silly
	Mellow	Disappointed	Touchy	Anxious	
		Dissatisfied	Resistant	Cautious	

INTENSITY OF FEELINGS

When I imagine my baby I see . . .

_____

_____

When I think about my baby I feel . . .

_____

_____

Remembering my baby helps . . .

_____

_____

I feel loved and cared for knowing . . .

_____

_____

When people ask me how I'm doing, I feel . . .

_____

_____

Sometimes I get tired of . . .

_____

_____

When I think about reuniting with my baby in heaven I feel . . .

_____

_____

My heart looks like this today...

Create a visual depiction with drawings, doodles, clip art, crayons, markers, words, quotes, or whatever helps you capture your heart in picture form.

LINGER IN GOD'S LIGHT

Jesus taught us by example to get out of the rat race and recharge our batteries.

BARBARA JOHNSON

Relax and Breathe

Settle into a quiet, comfortable place. Close your eyes and take in a deep breath, slowly over the course of four seconds. As you breathe in, invite God to permeate you with life-giving energy and peace. Hold your breath for four seconds, and then slowly exhale. Release all stress and nagging thoughts to God, allowing Him to take them for the time being.

Read

While you read the following scriptures out loud, the Holy Spirit will illumine your mind, highlighting certain ideas. Be attentive to the thoughts, pictures, and impressions that come to you. Circle the words and phrases that speak to you. Don't hurry. This is your time to linger in God's presence and receive what you need.

> Two others, both criminals, were led out to be executed with him (Jesus). When they came to a place called The Skull, they nailed him to the cross. And the criminals were also crucified—one on his right and one on his left.
> Jesus said, "Father, forgive them, for they don't know what they are doing." And the soldiers gambled for his clothes by throwing dice. The crowd watched and the leaders scoffed.
> "He saved others," they said, "Let him save himself if he is really God's Messiah, the Chosen One." The soldiers mocked him, too, by offering him a drink of sour wine.

They called out to him, "If you are the King of the Jews, save yourself!"
A sign was fastened above him with these words: "This is the King of the Jews."

One of the criminals hanging beside him scoffed, "So you're the Messiah, are you? Prove it by saving yourself—and us, too, while you're at it!"

But the other criminal protested, "Don't you fear God even when you have been sentenced to die? We deserve to die for our crimes, but this man hasn't done anything wrong." Then he said, "Jesus, remember me when you come into your Kingdom."

And Jesus replied, "I assure you, today you will be with me in paradise."

Luke 23:32-43 NLT

Without question, this is the great mystery of our faith:
Christ was revealed in a human body and vindicated by the Spirit.
He was seen by angels and announced to the nations.
He was believed in throughout the world and taken to heaven in glory.

1 Timothy 3:16 NLT

Paul said, "I will reluctantly tell about visions and revelations from the Lord. I was caught up to the third heaven fourteen years ago. Whether I was in my body or out of my body, I don't know—only God knows. Yes, only God knows whether I was in my body or outside my body. But I do know that I was caught up to paradise and heard things so astounding they cannot be expressed in words, things no human is allowed to tell. That experience is worth boasting about, but I'm not going to do it.

I will boast only about my weaknesses . . . even though I have received such wonderful revelations from God.

2 Corinthians 12:1-7 NLT

John the Apostle said, "Then I saw a new heaven and a new earth, for the old heaven and the old earth had disappeared. And the sea was also gone. And I saw the holy city, the New Jerusalem, coming down from God out of heaven like a bride beautifully dressed for her husband. I heard a loud shout from the throne, saying, "Look, God's home is now among his people! He will live with them, and they will be his people. God himself will be with them. He will wipe every tear from their eyes, and there will be no more death or sorrow or crying or pain. All these things are gone forever." And the one sitting on the throne said, "Look, I am making everything new!" And then he said to me, "Write this down, for what I tell you is trustworthy and true."

Revelation 21:1-5 NLT

Jesus said, "Seek the Kingdom of God above all else, and he will give you everything you need. So don't be afraid, little flock. For it gives your Father great happiness to give you the Kingdom."

Luke 12:31-32 NLT

When everything is ready, I will come and get you, so that you will always be with me where I am."

John 14:3 NLT

Reflect

What shines out to you? Why?

_____

Renew

Today I will be mindful of my baby in paradise. What comes to mind is . . .

_____

I will share these thoughts with . . .

_____

Release and Receive

Lord, today I release to You . . .

_____

I open my heart to receive from You . . .

_____

LOOK FOR THE GOOD

The road through the Valley of Shadows takes us through many unfamiliar places and experiences. We long for the familiar comfort of the way things were before our baby passed. It's just part of being human. And while we can acknowledge our longings with gentle compassion, healing comes by living in the moment and finding meaning in our loss.

When you think about your life, what positive gifts or changes have come to you as a consequence of your loss? Think in terms of your life goals, existing relationships and new ones that have formed as a result of your loss, the value or significance of your loss, and any other blessings that have come to you.

What gifts have come to me after my loss?

- _____
- _____
- _____
- _____

SEARCHING FOR POSITIVE CHANGE

Researchers asked 240 bereaved individuals to write for twenty minutes, three times in one week. Each group had a different focus: One group wrote about their deepest thoughts and feelings about their loss. Another was asked to focus on making sense of their loss by exploring possible causes and by writing about how the loss fit into their lives according to their assumptions about the way the world works. Another group was asked to focus their writing on any positive life changes that had come about as a result of their loss. Control group participants were asked to describe the room in which they were seated, and to minimize expression of emotion in their writing.

Physical health improved over time in all treatment groups, but three months after expressive writing, results showed that writing about loss experiences was more effective in reducing Prolonged Grief Disorder symptoms than writing about a neutral topic. The individuals who wrote about the meaning and positive elements discovered in grieving their loss showed the greatest decrease in depressive and Post-Traumatic Stress symptoms. Following traumatic loss, efforts to find meaning and to make sense of a loss was highly correlated with Post-Traumatic Growth and healthy adjustment.[76]

GIFTS & POSITIVE PERSPECTIVES PARENTS MENTION AFTER A LOSS

- I value life more. Life is greater than death.
- I am more aware of the impermanence of life.
- I better understand that there are no guarantees about when or how we die.
- I've grown in strength, maturity, and have re-arranged my priorities.
- I'm closer to my family and appreciate them more.
- I'm making better choices to take care of myself and practice healthy habits.
- I'm more patient and less easily upset by "small stuff" or "little things."
- I'm more accepting of myself and others.
- I appreciate others more and want to help those who have experienced painful events.
- I work harder at reaching out and building close relationships.
- I feel stronger and more capable of coping with difficult situations.
- I'm less afraid.
- I don't take things for granted like I did before,
- I tell others I appreciate them more.
- I'm more tuned in to others and have more empathy with them.
- I'm more intentional about finding meaning and purpose in my experiences. Either everything has meaning or nothing has meaning.
- I've discovered that the ability to feel deep emotion is a gift.
- I'm more open to new experiences, knowing life can be cut short.
- My relationship with God is much stronger. My faith is alive. I think often of eternity and a future reunion with my baby.
- I have more time and energy for other things.

- I'm more grateful for the generous love and support offered by family and/or friends.
- I believe our baby's brief presence in the world made a positive long-lasting impact.
- I've learned to be more accepting of life's imperfections, the inevitability of death, and the fragile nature of humanity.
- The bond with my baby lives on in spite of their absence. Love never dies.
- My baby is free from all human suffering.

LIFT UP THANKS

When life blindsides us and we are stripped of our sense of control, fear tends to drive our thoughts onto a negative track. Every time we repeat a negative thought, neural connections in the brain are strengthened. Cells that fire together, wire together. Think of it like ruts on a dirt road. Each time a car drives on a dirt road, the grooves get deeper and more entrenched. The longer we stay on a negative track, rehearsing everything that is bad about our situation, the more entrenched the negative thoughts become, making it more and more difficult to get off the track.

Lifting up thanks breaks us free from negative ruminations, helps us to remember God's goodness, and reconnects us with the positives in our life. Take a moment now and whisper words of thanks for some of the new perspectives and positive changes you've experienced in this season.

I'm thankful . . .

I'm thankful . . .

I'm thankful . . .

_____

I'll reward myself for persevering through grief by . . .

_____

I will invite _____ to share this reward with me.

_____

LIGHTEN YOUR LOAD

> *What lies behind us and what lies before us*
> *are tiny matters compared to what lies within us.*
> RALPH WALDO EMERSON

Write a love letter to your baby. There are no rights and wrongs on this. Simply use the letter as a way to tell your baby what you'd like him or her to know. You might consider sharing:

- how you feel about them

- your hopes for them

- your thoughts about seeing them again

- a thank you for the ways they have left a significant mark on you and others

- some words about what their life taught you and how you are different because of who they are.

Take your time. There is no rush. Some women like to write the letter over several days, adding content when new thoughts surface. Feel free to write your letter in whatever way seems best for you.

A Love Letter to My Baby

A Love Letter to My Baby (p. 2)

DAY NINETEEN
Being Your Best Self

TODAY'S READING
EMPTY ARMS | CHAPTER EIGHTEEN | PAGES 151–164

> *You gain strength, courage, and confidence by every experience in which you really stop and look fear in the face. You are able to say to yourself, "I've lived through this. . . I can take the next thing that comes along." You must do the thing you think you cannot do.*
>
> ELEANOR ROOSEVELT

Listen To Your Heart

You are developing a healthy lifetime habit of paying attention to your feelings, an important part of who you are and how you are designed. Birds fly. Fish swim. People feel. Feeling is healing. You name your feelings because when you name them, you can tame them, and let them go.

Take some time now to listen to what your heart has to say.

- Using the *Feelings* list on the next page, circle the feelings you experienced while reading chapter eighteen of *Empty Arms*.

- Draw a double circle around one or two feelings that are most intense or that seem to stay with you longer than others. On a scale of 1-10, with 10 being most intense, identify the level of intensity by writing a number to the right of each feeling you circled.

TODAY MY HEART IS SAYING...

My Feelings

	HAPPY	SAD	ANGRY	SCARED	ASHAMED
INTENSITY OF FEELINGS	**Excited**	**Depressed**	**Furious**	**Terrified**	**Defamed**
	Overjoyed	**Agonized**	**Enraged**	**Horrified**	**Remorseful**
	Elated	**Alone**	**Outraged**	**Scared stiff**	**Dishonored**
	Thrilled	**Hurt**	**Boiling**	**Fearful**	**Admonished**
	Fired Up	**Sorrowful**	**Irate**	**Panicky**	
		Miserable	**Seething**	**Shocked**	
	Gratified	Heartbroken	Upset	Apprehensive	Apologetic
	Cheerful	Somber	Mad	Frightened	Sneaky
	Satisfied	Lost	Defended	Insecure	Guilty
	Relieved	Distressed	Frustrated	Uneasy	Secretive
	Glowing	Melancholy	Agitated	Intimidated	
		Let Down	Disgusted	Threatened	
	Glad	Unhappy	Perturbed	Nervous	Ridiculous
	Pleasant	Moody	Annoyed	Worried	Regretful
	Tender	Blue	Uptight	Timid	Pitied
	Pleased	Upset	Irritated	Unsure	Silly
	Mellow	Disappointed	Touchy	Anxious	
		Dissatisfied	Resistant	Cautious	

It's hard for me to let go of . . .

_____

Letting go feels risky because . . .

_____

LINGER IN GOD'S LIGHT

Relax and Breathe

Inhale deeply, filling your lungs to capacity. Hold your breath for four seconds, then exhale very slowly. Notice the physical sensations of the air entering and exiting your body. With each breath, invite God's love and life-giving energy to calm and quiet your body. Exhale your tension. Inhale God's peace. Exhale stress. Repeat this inhale/exhale pattern four times as you prepare to receive from God.

Read

God's answer to your problems is, "Come to Me." God knows all the persistent thoughts that chip away at your peace. He is eager to meet with you. As you prepare to spend time together, invite the Holy Spirit to shine the spotlight on what will bring life and freedom. Slowly read the following scriptures out loud. Circle words and phrases that resonate with you. Be attentive to thoughts, pictures, and impressions that surface. Don't hurry. Linger and receive.

> After saying all these things, Jesus looked up to heaven and said, "Father, the hour has come. Glorify your Son so he can give glory back to you. For you have given him authority over everyone. He gives eternal life to each one you have given him. And this is the way to have eternal life—to know you, the only true God, and Jesus Christ, the one you sent to earth. I brought glory to you here

on earth by completing the work you gave me to do. Now, Father, bring me into the glory we shared before the world began.

"I have revealed you to the ones you gave me from this world. They were always yours. You gave them to me, and they have kept your word. Now they know that everything I have is a gift from you, for I have passed on to them the message you gave me. They accepted it and know that I came from you, and they believe you sent me.

"My prayer is not for the world, but for those you have given me, because they belong to you. All who are mine belong to you, and you have given them to me, so they bring me glory. Now I am departing from the world; they are staying in this world, but I am coming to you. Holy Father, you have given me your name; now protect them by the power of your name so that they will be united just as we are. During my time here, I protected them by the power of the name you gave me. I guarded them so that not one was lost, except the one headed for destruction, as the Scriptures foretold.

"Now I am coming to you. I told them many things while I was with them in this world so they would be filled with my joy. I have given them your word. And the world hates them because they do not belong to the world, just as I do not belong to the world. I'm not asking you to take them out of the world, but to keep them safe from the evil one. They do not belong to this world any more than I do. Make them holy by your truth; teach them your word, which is truth. Just as you sent me into the world, I am sending them into the world. And I give myself as a holy sacrifice for them so they can be made holy by your truth.

"I am praying not only for these disciples but also for all who will ever believe in me through their message. I pray that they will all be one, just as you and I are one—as you are in me, Father, and

I am in you. And may they be in us so that the world will believe you sent me.

"I have given them the glory you gave me, so they may be one as we are one. I am in them and you are in me. May they experience such perfect unity that the world will know that you sent me and that you love them as much as you love me. Father, I want these whom you have given me to be with me where I am. Then they can see all the glory you gave me because you loved me even before the world began!

"O righteous Father, the world doesn't know you, but I do; and these disciples know you sent me. I have revealed you to them, and I will continue to do so. Then your love for me will be in them, and I will be in them."

John 17:1-26 NLT

Leaving there, he went, as he so often did, to Mount Olives. The disciples followed him. When they arrived at the place, he said, "Pray that you don't give in to temptation."

He pulled away from them about a stone's throw, knelt down, and prayed, "Father, remove this cup from me. But please, not what I want. What do you want?" At once an angel from heaven was at his side, strengthening him. He prayed on all the harder. Sweat, wrung from him like drops of blood, poured off his face.

He got up from prayer, went back to the disciples and found them asleep, drugged by grief. He said, "What business do you have sleeping? Get up. Pray so you won't give in to temptation." No sooner were the words out of his mouth than a crowd showed up, Judas, the one from the Twelve, in the lead. He came right up to Jesus to kiss him. Jesus said, "Judas, you would betray the Son of Man with a kiss?"

When those with him saw what was happening, they said, "Master, shall we fight?" One of them took a swing at the Chief Priest's servant and cut off his right ear.

Jesus said, "Let them be. Even in this." Then, touching the servant's ear, he healed him.

Jesus spoke to those who had come—high priests, Temple police, religion leaders: "What is this, jumping me with swords and clubs as if I were a dangerous criminal? Day after day I've been with you in the Temple and you've not so much as lifted a hand against me. But do it your way—it's a dark night, a dark hour."

Luke 22:39-53 MSG

Jesus said, "I still have many things to tell you, but you can't handle them now. But when the Friend comes, the Spirit of the Truth, he will take you by the hand and guide you into all the truth there is. He won't draw attention to himself, but will make sense out of what is about to happen and, indeed, out of all that I have done and said. He will honor me; he will take from me and deliver it to you. Everything the Father has is also mine. That is why I've said, 'He takes from me and delivers to you'."

John 16:12-15 MSG

Reflect

What words, phrases, or ideas shine out to you? Why?

Renew

Write down one thought from the scriptures above to reflect on through the day.

I sense God saying to me . . .

One insight I'd like to share with a friend is . . .

Release and Receive

Lord, today I release to You . . .

I open my heart to receive from You . . .

LOOK FOR THE GOOD

Name three character strengths you see in Jesus from the scriptures you read today.

1. _____

2. _____

3. _____

What qualities in Jesus would you like the Holy Spirit to cultivate in you? Remember, nothing is impossible with God. How can you cooperate with God in process?

_____

_____

_____

BEING THE BEST YOU

People who daily participated in the Best Possible Self exercise for two weeks showed increases in positive emotions at the end of the two-week study. Those who continued the exercise following the study showed increases in positive mood one month later. The exercise asked participants to envision a brighter future and write down how they saw themselves. The benefits of this practice for you? Increased positive mood, greater awareness of what you want in life, and the chance to proactively prioritize and plan how to reach your goals.[77]

Now, take a moment to think forward five years. Envision the woman you want to be—you at your very best. Write down how you imagine yourself five years from now.

• What do you see?

_____

• What does the growth in your relationship with God look like?

_____

• How do you imagine yourself loving others?

_____

• How have you grown in loving *you*?

_____

• What character qualities shine in you?

_____

• How do you feel about what you see?

_____

> *Jesus said, "So, you believe because you've seen with your own eyes.*
> *Even better blessings are in store for those who*
> *believe without seeing."*
>
> JOHN 20:29 MSG

LIFT UP THANKS

When I think about all I've been through and survived, I want to thank God the Father for . . .

_____

I want to thank Jesus for . . .

_____

I want to thank the Holy Spirit for . . .

_____

LIGHTEN YOUR LOAD

Today I can show compassion toward myself by . . .

_____

Today I let go of pushing too hard and too fast. I will be less intense and ease up on myself by . . .

_____

_____

_____

_____

_____

DAY TWENTY
Honoring Your Progress

TODAY'S READING
EMPTY ARMS | EPILOGUE | PAGES 165-166

> *A miracle has been performed in us! We can be mindful of the awesome fact that God lives within us and finds great pleasure in who we are.*
>
> PAMELA REEVE

Listen To Your Heart

Healing requires us to stop traveling in five-speed overdrive and to turn down the noise. To move out of our heads and into our hearts. It may seem easier to deny, block, or repress our feelings, but denied feelings don't go away, they go underground, trapping us in grief.

You are building into your life an effective guard against prolonging your pain and complicating your recovery by daily creating a quiet, safe place to listen to what is going on inside, without criticism or judgment. It doesn't help to tell yourself, *You shouldn't feel that way. . . That's stupid . . . Don't be so immature.* It takes more energy to shame yourself than it does to simply acknowledge feelings without judgment, release them, and let them go.

Opening your heart in the light of God's love, and acknowledging *what is*, is far more productive than resisting and denying the messages of your heart. It empowers you to keep moving forward through your grief.

Take some time now to listen to what your heart has to say.

- Using the *Feelings* list on the next page, circle the feelings you experienced while reading the epilogue of *Empty Arms*.

- Draw a double circle around one or two feelings that are most intense or that seem to stay with you longer than others. On a scale of 1-10, with 10 being most intense, identify the level of intensity by writing a number to the right of each feeling you circled.

My Feelings

HAPPY	SAD	ANGRY	SCARED	ASHAMED
Excited	Depressed	Furious	Terrified	Defamed
Overjoyed	Agonized	Enraged	Horrified	Remorseful
Elated	Alone	Outraged	Scared stiff	Dishonored
Thrilled	Hurt	Boiling	Fearful	Admonished
Fired Up	Sorrowful	Irate	Panicky	
	Miserable	Seething	Shocked	
Gratified	Heartbroken	Upset	Apprehensive	Apologetic
Cheerful	Somber	Mad	Frightened	Sneaky
Satisfied	Lost	Defended	Insecure	Guilty
Relieved	Distressed	Frustrated	Uneasy	Secretive
Glowing	Melancholy	Agitated	Intimidated	
	Let Down	Disgusted	Threatened	
Glad	Unhappy	Perturbed	Nervous	Ridiculous
Pleasant	Moody	Annoyed	Worried	Regretful
Tender	Blue	Uptight	Timid	Pitied
Pleased	Upset	Irritated	Unsure	Silly
Mellow	Disappointed	Touchy	Anxious	
	Dissatisfied	Resistant	Cautious	

INTENSITY OF FEELINGS

My heart looks like this today . . .

Create a picture of your feelings below. Feel free to add color with pencils, markers, crayons, or create a collage of pictures and words clipped from a magazine.

LINGER IN GOD'S LIGHT

Relax and Breathe

Settle into a quiet, comfortable place. Close your eyes and take in a deep breath, slowly over the course of four seconds. As you breathe in, invite God to permeate you with life-giving energy and peace. Hold your breath for four seconds, and then slowly exhale. Release all stress and nagging thoughts to God, allowing Him to take them for the time being. Repeat this inhale/exhale pattern four times to quiet yourself and prepare to receive from God.

Read

While you read the following scriptures, the Holy Spirit will illumine your mind, highlighting certain ideas. Be attentive to the thoughts, pictures, and impressions that come to you. Circle the words and phrases that speak to you. Don't hurry. This is your time to linger in God's presence and receive what you need.

> I will lead them down a new path, guiding them along an unfamiliar way.
> I will brighten the darkness before them and smooth out the road ahead of them.
> Yes, I will indeed do these things; I will not forsake them.

Isaiah 42:16 NLT

> Do not forget GOD, your God, the God who led you through that huge and fearsome wilderness, those desolate, arid badlands . . . the God who gave you water gushing from hard rock; . . . so that you would be prepared to live well in the days ahead of you.

Deuteronomy 8:14-17 MSG

When the poor and needy search for water and there is none,
And their tongues are parched from thirst,
Then I, the LORD, will answer them.
I, the God of Israel, will never abandon them.
I will open up rivers for them on the high plateaus.
I will give them fountains of water in the valleys.
I will fill the desert with pools of water.
Rivers fed by springs will flow across the parched ground. . .
I am doing this so all who see this miracle
Will understand what it means—
That it is the LORD who has done this.

Isaiah 41:17-20 NLT

———————————

Encourage the exhausted, and strengthen the feeble.
Say to those with anxious heart,
"Take courage, fear not.
Behold, your God will come with vengeance;
The recompense of God will come,
He will save you."
Then the eyes of the blind will be opened
And the ears of the deaf will be unstopped.
Then the lame will leap like a deer,
And the tongue of the mute will shout for joy.
For waters will break forth in the wilderness
And streams in the Arabah.
The scorched land will become a pool
And the thirsty ground springs of water. . .

Isaiah 35:3-7 NASB

Reflect

What shines out to you? Why?

_____

Renew

Today I will be mindful of . . .

_____

I will share this with . . .

_____

Release and Receive

Lord, today I release to You . . .

_____

I open my heart to receive from You . . .

_____

LOOK FOR THE GOOD

Take a few moments to flip back through your journal. Look for ways you have grown and for positive changes that have come since your loss. What are the good things you notice about yourself? About your relationships? How do you feel about those positive changes?

- _____

- _____

- _____

LIFT UP THANKS

God has made everything beautiful for its own time. He has planted eternity in the human heart, but even so, people cannot see the whole scope of God's work from beginning to end. So I concluded there is nothing better than to be happy and enjoy ourselves as long as we can. And people should eat and drink and enjoy the fruits of their labor, for these are gifts from God.

ECCLESIASTES 3:11-13 NLT

I'm thankful for . . .

_____

I'm thankful because . . .

_____

I'm thankful to be . . .

_____

I can reward myself for the hard work of healthy grieving by . . .

_____

Who can I invite to share this reward with me?

_____

LIGHTEN YOUR LOAD

Write a letter to God. There are no right or wrong ways to approach this. Simply use the letter as a way to say the things you need to say. You might consider including:

- questions that continue to nag you

- how you feel about your relationship with God

- what you think and feel about the path you're on

- what you need and want more of now

- reasons you are thankful

- how God has made, and is making, a difference in your life.

Take your time. There is no rush. Some women like to write the letter over several days, adding content when new thoughts surface. Feel free to write your letter in whatever way seems best for you.

My Letter to God

_____

_____

_____

_____

_____

_____

_____

_____

_____

_____

_____

_____

_____

_____

_____

_____

DAY TWENTY-ONE
Rediscovering Joy

> *Joy is the serious business of Heaven.*
> C.S. LEWIS

Listen To Your Heart

Following my loss, a favorite chair in our living room became my secret place, where I lingered in God's presence. It was there that I faced my fears and doubts, asked God tough questions, listened, and took notes. The Holy Spirit helped me to grow in embracing the mystery and accepting the ambiguity of not having the answers I wanted. I'm not as far along as I'd like to be, but I'm further than I was. Dark shadows have a way of persistently reminding me, *God is God. You are not.*

Like you, I wanted to work through my grief so that I didn't get stuck in the shadows or drag the baggage of the present pain into the next season. I longed to exit the Valley of Death renewed and transformed, not just "all right." I yearned for the abundant joy and peace that Jesus promises in the Gospels. One thing was certain: I knew I couldn't turn my own mourning into dancing. I'd have to leave that up to Him.

I'm delighted to tell you that the Promise Keeper kept His promise. A wellspring of joy bubbles strong within me today. That doesn't mean my life is perfect. No, it's far from it. It does mean that life is full of joy in the midst of the difficult and messy. God knows how to care for His own. He taught me one step at a time how to pass through the searing pain of loss. Along the way He offered wonderful gifts for re-entering life on new terms.

What color are your feelings?

What might the color of joy in the midst
of the difficult look like to you?

Take some time now to listen to what your heart has to say.

- Using the *Feelings* list on the next page, circle the feelings you have now after reading *Empty Arms* and completing this journal.

- Draw a double circle around one or two feelings that are different than the ones you circled at the beginning of your process. On a scale of 1-10, with 10 being most intense, identify the level of intensity by writing a number to the right of each feeling you circled.

TODAY MY HEART IS SAYING...

My Feelings

INTENSITY OF FEELINGS

HAPPY	SAD	ANGRY	SCARED	ASHAMED
Excited	**Depressed**	**Furious**	**Terrified**	**Defamed**
Overjoyed	**Agonized**	**Enraged**	**Horrified**	**Remorseful**
Elated	**Alone**	**Outraged**	**Scared stiff**	**Dishonored**
Thrilled	**Hurt**	**Boiling**	**Fearful**	**Admonished**
Fired Up	**Sorrowful**	**Irate**	**Panicky**	
	Miserable	**Seething**	**Shocked**	
Gratified	Heartbroken	Upset	Apprehensive	Apologetic
Cheerful	Somber	Mad	Frightened	Sneaky
Satisfied	Lost	Defended	Insecure	Guilty
Relieved	Distressed	Frustrated	Uneasy	Secretive
Glowing	Melancholy	Agitated	Intimidated	
	Let Down	Disgusted	Threatened	
Glad	Unhappy	Perturbed	Nervous	Ridiculous
Pleasant	Moody	Annoyed	Worried	Regretful
Tender	Blue	Uptight	Timid	Pitied
Pleased	Upset	Irritated	Unsure	Silly
Mellow	Disappointed	Touchy	Anxious	
	Dissatisfied	Resistant	Cautious	

My heart looks like this today . . .

Create a visual display with drawings, doodles, clip art, crayons, markers, words, quotes, or whatever helps you capture your heart in picture form.

LINGER IN GOD'S LIGHT

The seed is in the ground.
Now may we rest in hope
while darkness does its work.

WENDELL BERRY

Relax and Breathe

Settle into a quiet, comfortable place. Close your eyes and take in a deep breath, slowly over the course of four seconds. As you breathe in, invite God to permeate you with life-giving energy and peace. Hold your breath for four seconds, and then slowly exhale. Release all stress and nagging thoughts to God, allowing Him to take them for the time being. Repeat this inhale/exhale pattern four times to quiet yourself and prepare to receive from from God.

Read

While you read the following scriptures slowly, out loud, the Holy Spirit will illumine your mind, highlighting certain ideas. Be attentive to the thoughts, pictures, and impressions that come to you. Circle the words and phrases that speak to you. Don't hurry. This is your time to linger in God's presence and receive what you need.

> Because you got a double dose of trouble and more than your share of contempt, Your inheritance in the land will be doubled and your joy go on forever.

Isaiah 61:6-7 MSG

Then those who feared the LORD spoke with each other, and the LORD listened to what they said. In his presence, a scroll of remembrance was written to record the names of those who feared him and always thought about the honor of his name. "They will be my people," says the LORD of Heaven's Armies.

Malachi 3:16-17 NLT

———————

And a great road will go through that once deserted land.
It will be named the Highway of Holiness.
It will be only for those who walk in God's ways;
fools will never walk there.
There will be no other dangers.
Only the redeemed will walk on it.
Those who have been ransomed by the LORD will return.
They will enter singing,
crowned with everlasting joy.
Sorrow and mourning will disappear,
and they will be filled with joy and gladness.

Isaiah 35:8-10 NLT

———————

But what happens when we live God's way? He brings gifts into our lives, much the same way that fruit appears in an orchard—things like affection for others, exuberance about life, serenity. We develop a willingness to stick with things, a sense of compassion in the heart, and a conviction that a basic holiness permeates things and people. We find ourselves involved in loyal commitments, not needing to force our way in life, able to marshal and direct our energies wisely.

Galatians 5:22-23 MSG

———————

No eye has seen, no ear has heard, and no mind has imagined what God has prepared for those who love him. But it was to us that God revealed these things by his Spirit. For his Spirit searches out everything and shows us God's deep secrets. No one can know a person's thoughts except that person's own spirit, and no one can know God's thoughts except God's own Spirit. And we have received God's Spirit (not the world's spirit), so we can know the wonderful things God has freely given us. When we tell you these things, we do not use words that come from human wisdom. Instead, we speak words given to us by the Spirit, using the Spirit's words to explain spiritual truths. But we understand these things, for we have the mind of Christ.

2 Corinthians 2: 9-16 NLT

THE BENEFITS OF WRITING

A written choice has power. A bundle of nerves at the base of your brain known as the RAS (Reticular Activating System), filters up to 2 million pieces of incoming data at any time from your five senses. When you write down your choices, you signal your brain that "this is important." The RAS then flags relevant options and ways to help you make that choice. More detailed choices create a pattern in your brain that it will more likely revert to later.[78]

Reflect

What shines out to you? Why?

_____

_____

_____

_____

Renew

Today I will be mindful of. . .

_____

_____

_____

_____

I will share these thoughts with . . .

_____

_____

Release & Receive

Lord, today I release to You . . .

_____

I open my heart to You to receive . . .

_____

LOOK FOR THE GOOD

> *Whatever is good and perfect is a gift coming down to us from God our Father, who created all the lights in the heavens. He never changes or casts a shifting shadow. He chose to give birth to us by giving us his true word. And we, out of all creation, became his prized possession.*
>
> JAMES 1:17-18 NLT

Name three good things that bring a smile to your face. What part did you play in those things coming to pass?

- _____
- _____
- _____

LIFT UP THANKS

If you tend to focus on things that aren't getting accomplished, it can block you from being thankful for the things that are going well and progress you've already made. Take a moment to notice what you *are* able to do now and how far you have come after your loss. Whisper a prayer of thanks for the growth you've experienced.

I'm thankful . . .

_____

I'm thankful . . .

_____

I'm thankful . . .

_____

To reward myself for making steps forward I will . . .

_____

_____

I will invite _____ to share this reward with me.

_____

LIGHTEN YOUR LOAD

You can lighten your load by planning and preparing for the days ahead. There are certain times in the next year that you'll want to create a plan to take very good care of you. Intense grief is often triggered by significant past dates and events.

SIGNIFICANT DATES THAT NEED A PLAN

- Your baby's original due date
- The anniversary of the day your baby died
- Your first birthday after your loss
- Mother's Day

- Father's Day
- October 15th – Pregnancy Loss Awareness Day in USA
- Holidays
- Pregnancy announcements – It can be helpful to preplan a response that "your best you" can give others, rather than trying to come up with something on the spot.
- Baby showers
- When other babies are born
- Children's birthday parties

WAYS TO TAKE GOOD CARE OF YOU

Here is a collection of suggestions for the days ahead that may contain triggers. Pages are provided in the back of the book for you to continue your story on these significant days.

- A few weeks before the anniversary of your loss, ask a couple of close friends to pray daily for you until the anniversary passes.

- Plan to share the day with someone.

- Plan something fun or soothing to look forward to on the anniversary date – manicure, pedicure, spa treatment, favorite food, movie, concert, museum, picnic, hike. Give something away, treat someone else to something you enjoy, plant flowers, participate in a charity walk, take the day off and go somewhere with someone you love, buy yourself something special, help a friend in need, send yourself or someone else flowers, just because you can.

- Celebrate those who have supported you or the people you most appreciate at this point in time. Write thank you notes acknowledging their kindness and what they mean to you. Bake, make, or buy something small and deliver it to say, *Thanks for being you.*

THIS IS NOT THE END OF YOUR STORY . . .

The stage is set to keep moving forward.

How you choose to reflect on and tell your story is important to your physical, mental, and spiritual well-being. In the here and now, the terrific pain of your loss is valid, indicating your deep love and the precious meaning of your baby's life. And, as you have discovered during the past twenty-one days, there is much more going on than the naked eye can see.

Following the loss of our baby, my own trek through the Valley of Shadows revealed an unanticipated, slow, internal dismantling of how I defined myself and my dreams attached to the future. I ached for children to love but had no guarantee that this longing would be fulfilled.

I recall the words of my mentor, who met with me once a month for many years until she passed away—still sharp as a tack, at ninety-five. In the comfort of her living room, she poured hot tea while I poured out the troubles of my heart. One afternoon, when shadows loomed especially dark, I shared something with her about a dismantling process I sensed going on inside me. She knew my story well.

Gently setting down her porcelain cup and saucer, she seemed to look straight through me. It was the same kind of look my grandmother used to give me—the look that said, *Honey, I REALLY want you to pay attention.* And with a tilt of her head she stated with the utmost confidence, "Pam, God never allows the breaking down of a vessel unless He intends to build it back up into something of greater value and capacity."

Instantly, I understood. She was challenging me to believe that the Holy Spirit was working deep inside me, beyond my puny discernment. She was encouraging me to rest in God's unconditional love and power to transform me in ways that exceeded my comprehension.

I've never forgotten those words. A few decades down the road, they ring more true to me now than when I first heard them. First I have to open my hands to let go of what I'm grasping. Then my empty hands can receive something new. First I lose my life, then I gain it. First death, then resurrection. It's the message of the cross. It's also a blueprint for transformation.

My point here is, *This is not the end of your story.* The best chapters are yet to come, for you and for your baby.

Perhaps it can help to think about it this way. If you were to pull back the curtain and view your time on earth from an eternal perspective, you might see a tiny dot on a never-ending line. The dot represents all the chapters in your life story, beginning to end. A very special chapter is dedicated to the loss of your baby.

In the later chapters, you notice a difference. The Valley of Shadows transformed you. It's obvious that you see with new eyes. You are free of old preoccupations. There is a delightful awareness of God's nearness. You find God's goodness in the common, ordinary scenes of daily life. Gratitude freely flows from your heart, spilling joy wherever you go. You discover that the gifts you received in the Valley travel with you into new chapters.

Five valuable treasures continue to weave in and out of your story.

The gift of pausing to *listen to your heart.* You pay attention to what your heart feels and give it a voice. You turn toward your pain and embrace it, rather than denying, blocking, or running from it. You're aware of the triggers and needs connected with your feelings and compassionately address them. You know deep inside that to feel is to heal. The benefit of this gift? A greater knowledge and appreciation of who you are and forward movement in the healing process.

The gift of *lingering in the Light.* You intuitively know you're powerless to heal the devastation inside, or to light your way through the vast black valley of death. There is an inner knowing that says, *This is way beyond me!* Legitimate needs renew your dependence on God, the power of the Holy Spirit who lives in you, and His sacred love letters found in Scripture. The Spirit nudges you often to live in the moment, to talk things over, and to sort things out with the One who loves you relentlessly, rather than trying to do things on your own. The benefit of this gift? An ever unfolding love story.

Another gift you carried out of the bleak wilderness is a natural predisposition to *look for the good*. Why do you do this? Because you can. Because good surrounds you all day, every day, ready to be noticed and enjoyed. Because being mindful of the good serves up a sip of cool, refreshing water in a blistering wasteland. Because God is good, and the Giver of all good gifts. He has given you all things to enjoy and is present in your joy. The word *enjoy* literally means en (*in*) joy. The benefit to you? Relief from pain, and a sense of well-being in the midst of suffering.

Your grateful heart was also forged in that sad valley. *Lifting up thanks* for the good and lovely things in your life disarms discouragement, drives out despair, and serves as a healing salve for heartbreaking loss. It is necessary medicine during grief, simply to stabilize and regain sanity. Joy follows closely on the heels of gratitude. When the heart mends little by little, so, too, gratitude becomes more and more natural. Spontaneous thanks effortlessly bubbles up and out of you. You're more comfortable with your unique combination of strengths and weaknesses, and you treat yourself like God does, with more compassion and unconditional love.

And finally, you exited the valley with the gift of permission. You let go of having to do so much, and you give yourself grace. You now know, and I mean *really* know, that when life hits you like a freight train and dumps you into a valley of death, *lightening your load* isn't simply a nice idea; it's an absolute essential for healing after loss. So, you travel lightly by choosing to release your grip and let go of unrealistic expectations. You take risks by inviting God and safe friends to share the heavy weight of grief. You leave behind the tendency to appear like you're "fine" when you aren't, and you conserve energy by letting go of denial, pretending, and resisting the reality of *what is*. You prefer living freely out in the open. The benefit? Emotional freedom, deeper relationships, and increased energy to heal.

You've also cultivated an eternal perspective. Things can take on new meaning when we consider this life as a millisecond compared to the endless years of eternity. Between now and then, we are being prepared for the reality of heaven. My mentor used to tell me, "God will use all the events from the smallest to the largest, from the happiest to the most horrific, to prepare you for your place in heaven."

I'd like to ask you to do something. Will you take some time to glance back through your journal? You've come a long way from the place you began. Like a row of dominoes, the loss of your baby set off a series of questions, lessons, and valuable discoveries. It also opened the door to new beginnings.

Sometime soon, I hope you'll select one or two meaningful insights from each day in your *Empty Arms Journal*. Pick key ideas you want to remember going forward. Then fill up the Supersized Sticky Note that follows with your top takeaways. While you're at it, please lift up thanks. Take time to revel in your progress and share with someone special how you've grown. You've worked hard and deserve to enjoy the hard won spoils of victory. Even as you rightfully grieve, please celebrate each step forward and rejoice in every new beginning.

I deeply appreciate the feedback I receive from my readers. It helps others to make an informed decision before buying my book. If you found value in the *Empty Arms Journal*, would you please leave a brief review at the following link: http://a.co/9AWv2Cf

My top takeaways...

Reflections on my original due date . . .

_____

_____

_____

_____

_____

_____

_____

_____

_____

_____

_____

_____

_____

_____

_____

_____

_____

_____

_____

_____

_____

_____

_____

_____

_____

Reflections on the anniversary
of my baby's passing . . .

My reflections on Mother's day. . .

My reflections on Father's day . . .

My reflections on my birthday . . .

My reflections on October 15, National Pregnancy Loss Awareness day . . .

My reflections during the holidays . . .

My reflections during the holidays . . .

Meaningful ways people have expressed their love & support . . .

Meaningful ways people have expressed their love & support . . .

Endnotes

INTRODUCTION

1. Stephen Lepore, and M. A. Greenberg, "Mending broken hearts: Effects of expressive writing on mood, cognitive processing, social adjustment and health following a relationship breakup," *Psychology and Health, 17* (2002) pp. 547-560.

2. J. M. Smyth and M. A. Greenberg, "Scriptotherapy: the effects of writing about traumatic events," In Maslig, J. and Duberstien, P. (Ed.s) *Empirical Studies in Psychoanalytic Theories, 9: Psychoanalytic Perspectives on Health Psychology* (Washington, DC: American Psychological Association 2000) pp. 121-164.

3. J. W. Pennebaker, J. K. Kiecolt-Glaser and R. Glaser, "Disclosure of traumas and immune function. Health implications for psychotherapy," *Journal of Consulting and Clinical Psychology*, 56 (1988) pp. 239–245.

4. Lepore, Stephen J. Expressive writing moderates the relation between intrusive thoughts and depressive symptoms. *Journal of Personality and Social Psychology*, Nov 1997, Vol 73(5), 1030-1037.

5. P. Ullrich and S. Lutgendorf, "Journaling about stressful events: Effects of cognitive processing and emotional expression," *Annals of Behavioral Medicine, 24*(3) (2002, February) pp. 244-250.

6. Pennebaker, James W., and Colder, Michelle and Sharp, Lisa K. *Accelerating the coping process. Journal of Personality and Social Psychology,* Vol 58(3), Mar 1990, 528-537.

7. Drake Baer, "Expressive writing is a super easy way to become way happier," *Business Insider* (May 23, 2014). Retrieved from www.businessinsider.com/the-positive-effects-of-journaling-and-expressive-writing-2014-5.

8. H. G. Prigerson, M. J. Horowitz, S. C. Jacobs, et al. "Prolonged grief disorder: Psychometric validation of criteria proposed for DSM-V and ICD-11," *PLoS Med*, 2009;6:e1000121.

DAY I

9. P. A. Boelen, J. De Keijser, M. A. Van Den Hout and J. Van Den Bout, "Treatment of complicated grief: A comparison between cognitive-behavioral

therapy and supportive counseling," *Journal of Consulting and Clinical Psychology,* *75,* (2007) pp. 277–284. doi: www.dx.doi.org/10.1037/0022-006X.75.2.277

10. N.M. Simon, "Treating complicated grief." *JAMA: The Journal of the American Medical Association.* 2013;310:416–423. doi: www.dx.doi.org/10.1001/jama.2013.8614.

11. S. A. Gutman and V. P. Schindler, "The neurological basis of occupation," *Occupational Therapy International, 14*(2) (2007) pp. 71-85.

DAY 2

12. R. M. Stirtzinger, G. E. Robinson, D. E. Stewart and E. Ralevski, "Parameters of grieving in spontaneous abortion," *The International Journal of Psychiatry in Medicine, 29* (2) (1999) pp. 235-49.

13. S. X. Lin and J. N. Lasker, "Patterns of grief reaction after pregnancy loss," *American Journal of Orthopsychiatry* 66 (1996) pp. 262–271.

14. H. L. Stuckey and J. Nobel, "The connection between art, healing, and public health: A review of current literature," *American Journal of Public Health, 100*(2) (2010) pp. 254–263.

15. Ford Cannon, *Bodily Changes In Pain, Hunger, Fear, And Rage: An Account Of The Recent Researches Into The Function Of Bodily Excitement,* (New York: D. Appleton and Company, 1927). The fight-or-flight response was first coined by Walter B. Cannon, MD, at Harvard Medical School in the 1920s. It is also known as the fight, flight, freeze, or fawn response in PTSD, hyperarousal, or the acute stress response. It is simply the physiological reaction that occurs in our body in response to a perceived harmful event, attack, or threat to survival.

16. R.K. Wallace, H. Benson, A.F. Wilson, *A Wakeful Hypometabolic Physiological State.* American Journal of Physiology, September 1971, Vol. 221, pp. 795-799).

17. G. Fricchione, M. Nakao, P. Myers, P. C. Zuttermeister, M. Baim, C. L. Mandle, C. Medich, "Anxiety is a good indicator for somatic symptom reduction through behavioral medicine intervention in a mind/body medicine clinic," *Psychotherapy and Psychosomatics, 70,* 2001) pp. 50–57.

18. Kathleen Totter, "Four ways to 'relearn' your breathing technique for improved overall health" in *Global Health Advisor* (Toronto: ON Canada: Phillip Crawley, Publisher. *The Globe and Mail Inc., M5V 2S9.* Nov. 18, 2015). Retrieved from

www.theglobeandmail.com/life/health-and-fitness/health-advisor/four-ways-to-relearn-your-breathing-technique-for-improved-overall-health/article27321412

19. W. Cheyne McCallum, "The neurophysiology of attention," In *Encyclopedia Britannica* (2016). Retrieved from www.britannica.com/topic/attention/The-neurophysiology-of-attention.

20. Martin E. P. Seligman and Tracy A. Steen, "Positive psychology progress empirical validation of interventions," *American Psychologist* (2005, July/August) pp. 410-421.

21. Mei-Yee, Wing-Sze Wong, "The differential effects of gratitude and sleep on psychological distress in patients with chronic pain," *J Health Psychol*, February 2013, vol. 18 no. 2, pp. 263-271.

22. Spiros Zodhiates, *The Complete Word Study Dictionary: New Testament.* Chattanooga, TN: AMG Publishers, 2000.

23. Blair Justice, *A Different Kind Of Health: Finding Well-Being Despite Illness* (Houston, Texas: Peak Press 1998) pp. 100-101.

DAY 3

24. P. D. Blasio, E. Camisasca, S. C. Caravita, C. Ionio, L. Milani, and G. G. Valtolina, "The Effects of Expressive writing on postpartum depression and posttraumatic stress symptoms," *Psychological Report* 117(3) (Dec 2015) pp. 856-82.

25. R. A. Emmons and M. E. McCullough, "Counting blessings versus burdens: An experimental investigation of gratitude and subjective well-being in daily life," *Journal of Personality and Social Psychology*, 84 (2003) pp. 377–389.

26. A. Kersting, R. Dölemeyer, J. Steinig, F. Walter, K. Kroker, K. Baust and B. Wagner, "Brief Internet-based intervention reduces posttraumatic stress and prolonged grief in parents after the loss of a child during pregnancy: a randomized controlled trial," *Psychotherapy Psychosomatics Journal* 82(6) (2013) pp. 372-81.

DAY 4

27. Ephesians 4:26

28. C. VanOyen Witvliet, N. J. DeYoung, A. J. Hofelich and P. A. DeYoung, "Compassionate reappraisal and emotion suppression as alternatives to offense-

focused rumination: Implications for forgiveness and psychophysiological well-being," *The Journal of Positive Psychology* 6(4) (2011) pp. 286-299.

29. M. C. Eisma, M. S. Stroebe, H. A. W. Schut, W. Stroebe, B. Wolfgang, P. A. Boelen, and J. Van den Bout, "Avoidance processes mediate the relationship between rumination and symptoms of complicated grief and depression following loss," *Journal of Abnormal Psychology*, Vol 122(4), (Nov 2013): pp. 961-970.

30. Paul K. Piff, Pia Dietze, Matthew Feinberg, Daniel M. Stancato and Dacher Keltner, "Awe, the small self, and prosocial behavior," *Journal of Personality and Social Psychology*, Vol 108(6), (Jun 2015): pp. 883-899.

31. For more creative ideas for an awe walk go to Greater Good Science Center's Greater Good In Action website. www.ggia.berkeley.edu/practice/awe_walk

32. L.B. Shapira, and M. Mongrain, "The benefits of self-compassion and optimism exercises for individuals vulnerable to depression," *Journal of Positive Psychology*, 5, (2010) pp. 377-389.

DAY 5

33. J. Cacciatore, J. F. Froen and M. Killian, "Condemning-Self, Condemning-other: blame and mental health in women suffering stillbirth," *Journal of Mental Health Counselling* 5(4) (2013) pp. 342–359.

34. R. A. Emmons and M. E. McCullough, "Counting blessings versus burdens: An experimental investigation of gratitude and subjective well-being in daily life," *Journal of Personality and Social Psychology*, 84 (2003) pp. 377–389.

35. B. Shahar, O. Szsepsenwol, S. Zilcha-Mano, N. Haim, O. Zamir, S. Levi-Yeshuvi and N. Levit-Binnun, "A wait-list randomized controlled trial of loving-kindness meditation program for self-criticism," *Clinical Psychology Psychotherapy* 22(4) (2015 Jul-Aug) pp. 346-56.

DAY 6

36. Thomas Baumgartner, Markus Heinrichs, Aline Vonlanthen, Urs Fischbacher, Ernst Fehr. "Oxytocin Shapes the Neural Circuitry of Trust and Trust Adaptation in Humans". *Neuron*, Volume 58, Issue 4 , 639 – 650.

37. Rev. 12:17

38. Deut. 20:3-4 NLT

39. Hebrews 7:25 NLT

40. N. Park, C. Peterson, & M.E.P. Seligman, "Strengths of character and well-being." *Journal of Social and Clinical Psychology, 23* , (2004) pp. 603–619.

41. J. C. Huffman, C. M. DuBois, B. C. Healy, J. K. Boehm, T. B. Kashdan, C. M. Celano, J. W. Denninger, and S. Lyubomirsky, "Feasibility and utility of positive psychology exercises for suicidal inpatients," *General Hospital Psychiatry* 36(1) (Jan-Feb 2014) pp. 88-94.

42. Rom. 5:6-8

43. Eph. 2:4-6

44. I Cor. 6:19

45. Col 2:13-15

46. Heb. 2:14-15

47. 2 Tim. 1:7

48. Eph. 4:26-27

49. Luke 10:19

DAY 7

50. Maud Purcell, "The Health Benefits of Journaling", www.PsychCentral.com (October 30, 2015).

51. A. Newberg, E. D'Aquili, and V. Raise, *Why God Won't Go Away: Brain Science and the Biology of Belief* (New York: Ballentine, 2002) page 7.

DAY 8

52. M. H. Manser, *Dictionary of Bible Themes: The Accessible and Comprehensive Tool for Topical Studies.* (London: Martin Manser, 2009). Scripture index 8030.

53. W. G. Lichtenthal, J. M. Currier, R. A. Neimeyer, and N. J. Keesee, "Sense and significance: A mixed methods examination of meaning making after the loss of one's child," *Journal of Clinical Psychology* 66(7) (2010): pp. 791–812.

54. L. G. Calhoun, R. G. Tedeschi, A. Cann and E. A. Hank"s, Positive outcomes following bereavement: Paths to posttraumatic growth," *Psychological Belgica* 50, (2010) pp. 125-143.

55. Philip C. Watkins, *Gratitude and the Good Life,* (Netherlands: Springer, 2014) pp. 159-174.

DAY 9

56. Kristine Neff, "Tips for Practicing Self-Compassion," Retrieved from www.self-compassion.org/tips-for-practice/

57. J. O'Leary and C. Thorwick, "Fathers' perspectives during pregnancy, postperinatal loss," *Journal of Obstetric, Gynecologic, & Neonatal Nursing* 35 (2006) pp. 78–86.

58. P. Avelin, I. Radestad, K. Saflund, R. Wredling, and K. Erlandsson, "Parental grief and relationships after the loss of a stillborn baby," *Midwifery* 29 (2013) pp. 668–673.

59. Brown-Bowers, S. J. Fredman, S. G. Wanklyn, and C. M. Monson, "Cognitive-behavioral conjoint therapy for posttraumatic stress disorder: application to a couple's shared traumatic experience," *Journal of Clinical Psychology* 68(5) (May 2012) pp. 536-47.

60. T. M. C. Lee, M. Leung, W. Hou et al., *Distinct neural activity associated with focused-attention meditation and lovingkindness meditation,* PLoS ONE, vol. 7, no. 8, Article ID e40054, 2012.

61. S. Sears and S. Kraus, *I think therefore I am: Cognitive distortions and coping style as mediators for the effects of mindfulness meditation on anxiety, positive and negative affect, and hope.* Journal of Clinical Psychology, vol. 65, no. 6, pp. 561–573, 2009.

DAY 11

62. Matthew Killingsworth and Daniel Gilbert, "A Wandering Mind is an Unhappy Mind," *Science* 330(6006) (2010): p. 932.

63. Adam S. Radomsky, A.S., Alcolado,G.M., Abramowitz,J.S., Alonso,P., Belloch, A., Bouvard, M., Clark, D.A., Coles, M.E., Doron, G., Fernández-Álvarez, H. *You Can Run but You Can't Hide: Intrusive Thoughts on Six Continents.* Journal of Obsessive-Compulsive and Related Disorders 3, no.3 (2014): 269-279.

DAY 12

64. Shelley L. Kerr, Analise O'Donovan , Christopher A. Pepping. *Can Gratitude and Kindness Interventions Enhance Well-Being in a Clinical Sample?* Journal of Happiness Studies. February 2015, Volume 16, Issue 1, pp 17-36.

65. P. R. Goldin, K. McRae, W. Ramel, and J. J. Gross, *The neural bases of emotion regulation: reappraisal and suppression of negative emotion,* Biological Psychiatry, vol. 63, no. 6, pp. 577–586, 2008.

DAY 13

66. H.L. Willmington, *Willmington's Book of Bible Lists*, (Wheaton, IL: Tyndale, 1987) p. 133.

DAY 14

67. Jennifer Daubenmier, Jean Kristeller, Frederick M. Hecht, Nicole Maninger, Margaret Kuwata, Kinnari Jhaveri, Robert H. Lustig, … "Mindfulness Intervention for Stress Eating to Reduce Cortisol and Abdominal Fat among Overweight and Obese Women: An Exploratory Randomized Controlled Study," *Journal of Obesity* Volume 2011.

68. Mason, Epel, Aschbacher, Lustig, Acree, Kristeller, Cohn, Dallman, Moran, Bacchetti, Laraia, Hecht, Daubenmier, "Reduced reward-driven eating accounts for the impact of a mindfulness-based diet and exercise intervention on weight loss: Data from the SHINE (Supporting Health by Integrating Nutrition and Exercise) randomized controlled trial," *Appetite* 100 (May 1, 2016) pp. 86-93.

DAY 15

69. M. S. Nokia, S. Lensu, J.P. Ahtiainen, P.P. Johansson, L.G. Koch, S.L. Britton, and H. Kainulainen, "Physical exercise increases adult hippocampal neurogenesis in male rats provided it is aerobic and sustained," *Journal of Physiology* 594 (2016) pp. 1855–1873.

70. Richard J. Maddock, Gretchen A. Casazza, Dione H. Fernandez, and Michael I. Maddock. "Acute Modulation of Cortical Glutamate and GABA Content by Physical Activity," *The Journal of Neuroscience* 36(8) (February 24, 2016) pp. 2449-2457; doi:10.1523/JNEUROSCI.3455-15.2016.

71. R.A. Emmons, and M.E. McCullough, M. E., Op. cit.

DAY 16

72. Jeff C. Huffman, M.D., Christina M. DuBois, B.A., Brian C. Healy, Ph.D. , Julia K. Boehm, Ph.D. , Todd B. Kashdan, Ph.D. , Christopher M. Celano, M.D., John W. Denninger, M.D., Ph.D., Sonja Lyubomirsky, "Feasibility and utility of positive psychology exercises for suicidal inpatients." *General Hospital Psychiatry* 36 (2014) 88–94.

DAY 17

73. E.E. Carpenter, and P.W. Comfort, In *Holman Treasury of Key Bible Words: 200 Greek and 200 Hebrew Words Defined and Explained*, (Nashville, TN: Broadman & Holman Publishers, 2000) pp. 123–124.

74. J.H. Fowler, and N.A. Christakis, Nicholas, "The Dynamic Spread of Happiness In a Large Social Network: Longitudinal Analysis Over 20 Years in the Framingham Heart Study," *British Medical Journal* 337(a2338) (2008) pp. 1-9. Retrieved from www.jhfowler.ucsd.edu/dynamic_spread_of_happiness.pdf.

75. J. Holt-Lunstad, T.B. Smith, and J.B. Layton, "Social Relationships and Mortality Risk: A Meta-analytic Review," *PLoS Med* 7(7) (2010): e1000316. doi:10.1371/journal.pmed.1000316.

DAY 18

76. W. G. Lichtenthal, and D. G. Cruess, "Effects of Directed Written Disclosure on Grief and Distress Symptoms Among Bereaved Individual," *Death Studies*, 34(6) (2010) pp. 475–499.

DAY 19

77. K. M. Sheldon, and S. Lyubomirsky, "How to increase and sustain positive emotion: The effects of expressing gratitude and visualizing best possible selves," *Journal of Positive Psychology* 1(2), 2006) pp. 73-82.

DAY 21

78. W. Cheyne McCallum. Op. cit.

240

ABOUT THE AUTHOR

Pam's reputation as a sought-after counselor, popular conference speaker, and best-selling author is built on her ability to explore real life issues with authenticity, warmth, and humor. Compelling stories, engaging faith, and perceptive insight give Pam the rare ability to inspire and empower audiences with practical tools for long lasting change.

Pam is married to her best friend, John, and has four children. Two reside in the United States, two are in heaven. During the last 25 years Pam has served thousands of individuals as a professional counselor in private practice. Coming along side those in the depths of pain, she has walked with them on the path of healing. Her grace-filled wisdom, refreshing hope, and practical counsel have guided many towards complete recovery.

For more helpful tools, encouragement, and free book give-aways
connect with Pam at:
www.pamvredevelt.com
and
www.facebook.com/authorpamvredevelt